# LIFE

# The Year in Pictures

## 2003

Tim Sloan/AFP

**As evening descends on the Iraqi town of Basra on April 19, the sky is displaced by a common product of modern war: thick, black, oily smoke.**

# LIFE

# The Year in Pictures

# LIFE

**Editor** Robert Sullivan
**Creative Director** Ian Denning
**Picture Editor** Barbara Baker Burrows
**Executive Editor** Robert Andreas
**Associate Picture Editor** Christina Lieberman
**Writer-Reporters** Hildegard Anderson (Chief), Carol Vinzant
**Copy** JC Choi (Chief), Mimi McGrath, Wendy Williams
**Production Manager** Michael Roseman
**Picture Research** Rachel Hendrick, Lauren Steel
**Photo Assistant** Joshua Colow
**Consulting Picture Editor (London)** Suzanne Hodgart

**Publisher** Andrew Blau
**Director of Business Development** Marta Bialek
**Business Manager** Craig Ettinger
**Assistant Finance Manager** Karen Tortora

**Editorial Operations** Richard K. Prue (Director), Richard Shaffer (Manager), Brian Fellows, Raphael Joa, Stanley E. Moyse (Supervisors), Keith Aurelio, Gregg Baker, Charlotte Coco, Scott Dvorin, Kevin Hart, Rosalie Khan, Po Fung Ng, Barry Pribula, David Spatz, Vaune Trachtman, Sara Wasilausky, David Weiner

**Time Inc. Home Entertainment**

**President** Rob Gursha
**Vice President, Branded Businesses** David Arfine
**Vice President, New Product Development** Richard Fraiman
**Executive Director, Marketing Services** Carol Pittard
**Director, Retail & Special Sales** Tom Mifsud
**Director of Finance** Tricia Griffin
**Assistant Marketing Director** Ann Marie Doherty

**Prepress Manager** Emily Rabin
**Book Production Manager** Jonathan Polsky
**Associate Product Manager** Jennifer Dowell

Special thanks to Bozena Bannett, Alex Bliss, Bernadette Corbie, Robert Dente, Gina Di Meglio, Anne-Michelle Gallero, Peter Harper, Suzanne Janso, Robert Marasco, Natalie McCrea, Mary Jane Rigoroso, Steven Sandonato, Grace Sullivan

As she gazes skyward in this scene from 1934's *Spitfire,* Katharine Hepburn is appearing in only her fifth motion picture, but already she exudes the special aura that made her a one-of-a-kind actress.

Published by

**LIFE** Books

Time Inc.
1271 Avenue of the Americas,
New York, NY 10020

ISBN: 1-931933-90-1
ISSN: 1092-0463
"LIFE" is a trademark of Time Inc.

We welcome your comments and suggestions
about LIFE Books. Please write to us at:
LIFE Books, Attention: Book Editors,
PO Box 11016, Des Moines, IA 50336-1016

If you would like to order any of our hardcover
Collector's Edition books, please call us at 1-800-
327-6388 (Monday through Friday, 7:00 a.m.–8:00
p.m. or Saturday, 7:00 a.m.–6:00 p.m. Central Time).

Please visit us, and sample past
editions of LIFE, at www.LIFE.com.

Iconic images from the LIFE Picture Collection are now available
as fine art prints and posters. The prints are reproductions on archival,
resin-coated photographic paper, framed in black wood, with an acid-
free mat. Works by the famous LIFE photographers—Eisenstaedt,
Parks, Bourke-White, Burrows, among many others—are available.
The LIFE poster collection presents large-format, affordable, suitable-
for-framing images. For more information on the prints, priced at
$99 each, call 888-933-8873, or go to www.purchaseprints.com.
The posters may be viewed and ordered at www.LIFEposters.com.

Ben Carbonetto Collection

# Whu Are the Heroes?

In a year filled with events of operatic grandeur and drama, observers were left to decide for themselves, and their decisions were important: What does it mean? What is good or bad? Who is right or wrong?

The President signals victory. Vanessa and Kobe Bryant face the press. Bethany Hamilton, before the incident, rides high.

T he country went to war in 2003, and therefore this was destined to be a year marked by bravery, despair, valor, heartbreak, heroism. As events unfurled, these amplified aspects of the human condition did come into play, at home as well as in Iraq, but seldom were they unshaded by questions. The year was one of great moment and force, yes, but it was also a year of ambiguities.

It begins with the war. There were questions about invading Iraq, but invade we did, and the march to Baghdad was stunning in its swiftness and efficiency. The regime of the malevolent Saddam Hussein, persecutor of his own people and others, was ended—and whether or not the battle should have been joined, and whether or not his removal was the reason for fighting (Was it to eliminate weapons of mass destruction? Was it to combat terrorism? Was it about oil?), most agreed the world was well rid of Saddam's rule. That he was not dead

at war's end dogged U.S. officials for eight long months in the way that Osama bin Laden, whose al-Qaeda organization showed signs of resurgence during the year, continued to dog them.

*War's end.* Did it end? More U.S. forces were killed in the weeks and months after President Bush donned a flight suit and declared an end to the fighting than had been during the monthlong campaign. What was the Coalition's plan for rebuilding Iraq? What was the plan for the peace? Bush cut a heroic figure when he addressed those servicemen and women, but when the Red Cross pulled workers out in the autumn because the situation had become too dangerous, and when searches failed to turn up weapons of mass destruction, many started to wonder what was going on. If Saddam's capture in December answered one big question, the world still remained a jittery place.

The year was infected by a lack of clarity, which, as it might in a year when we went to war, distressed the notion of "the hero." The President, dynamic and dressed for fight, was the very image of a hero—but was he a hero? Was Pfc. Jessica Lynch a hero or a victim? Dismiss for a moment any qualms about the war, and all the young men and women who fought for their country were heroes, as were all the brave soldiers of yore. But many of

**On October 29, nine major fires and eight smaller offshoots are being fought in California by 12,000 men and women—including these, in Simi Valley, heroes all. We needed heroes in this confusing year, and found them in fact and fiction. Our children found one in a fish named Nemo.**

us could not dismiss our qualms. This was unfair to those in the field. A medic cradling an Iraqi girl who had, moments before, become an orphan when her mother was caught in a cross fire—this man, who came out of his assignment to show compassion, to do something necessary, the pain of life in his downcast face—he was a hero, surely. Wasn't he?

We agreed on little. Basketball star Kobe Bryant was cheered as he appeared for a hearing on sexual assault charges in Colorado. To the kids who adored him: a hero fallen, or a hero still? Arnold Schwarzenegger played a hero, albeit a violent one, many times. Were people voting for the hero or the admittedly flawed human being? It was confusing.

In a few instances, we had heroes to trust. Bethany Hamilton, the 13-year-old surfer from Hawaii, was stoic when a shark bit off her arm. Her friends were resolute in applying the tourniquet and got her ashore: heroes all. The California firefighters: heroes all. We

craved heroes, and found them where we could.

There was that one . . . the one who captivated us, compelled us, drew us in—the one who needed to get home (as if from the fires, as if from the war), the one whose father was as brave and unremitting as he, the one whom we needed so badly in this year of ambiguity, the one who set the fish free! What was his name? Yes, that's right: Nemo.

You say he wasn't real? What was, in 2003?

Disney/Pixar

# Winter

## A Storm—and a Calm—Before a Larger Storm

On February 7, a storm beset Washington, D.C.—a city that knows how to handle many things but cannot handle snow—with a half foot of the white stuff. Nature created this tableau at 1600 Pennsylvania Avenue, as the work of the nation paused. The silence belied the urgency that was general throughout the land. The intention to go to war had been made clear to Iraq, and mobilization plans were in full effect. More than snow would soon fall.

**Photograph by Ron Edmons/AP**

## Hot Water

Ah yes, life is good for this snow monkey, lazing about in the soothing mineral waters of Shiga Kogen, located on a volcano in central Japan. These are the only hot springs in the world frequented by monkeys, and these Japanese macaques, as they are properly known, have been coming here for a long time. But all is not bliss for this species. While the monkey plays an important role in the Japanese imagination, deforestation is driving the animals more and more into paths of conflict with human beings, leading to friction in suburbs and on farms. Thus, even though these macaques are protected, about 5,000 of them are being killed each year, leaving at best 50,000 alive.

**Photograph by Kimimasa Mayama**
Reuters

**Jan. 9** A vessel appears off the coast of Australia bearing an Indonesian flag, tons of rotting fish, seven toothbrushes—but no crew. The 65-foot **"ghost ship,"** which may have been set on by pirates or mutineers, baffles authorities.

**Jan. 11** Outgoing Illinois Governor George Ryan **empties the state's death row.** He pardons four men condemned to die and commutes the death sentences of all the other 167 inmates to life in prison. Ryan calls Illinois's system of capital punishment "arbitrary and capricious, and therefore immoral." From 1977 to '99, the state had 12 executions and 13 exonerations.

**Jan. 13** The discovery of three hitherto unknown **moons around Neptune** is announced by astronomers at the Harvard-Smithsonian Center for Astrophysics, boosting to 11 the number of identified satellites orbiting the planet. The moons are so small and dimly lit that our eyes would have to be 100 million times more efficient to see them unaided.

## Fun Turns to Horror

On February 17, twenty-one people were killed and more than 50 injured in a stampede in a Chicago nightclub. Three days later, a fire resulting from the pyrotechnic display of the rock band Great White tears through a club in West Warwick, R.I. In this melee (right) and its aftermath, 100 die and 208 are injured. In both cases, the authorities, club owners and parents pointed fingers and placed blame; all of it will be sorted out in court cases. "What do you say? 'Gee, I'm sorry'?" asked Jack Russell, lead singer of Great White, whose guitarist was killed. "That just doesn't cut it . . . right now. I'm devastated."

**Photograph by Davidson Dan** Gamma

> **" We are fully engulfed, fully engulfed . . . We have people on fire inside. "**
>
> —**Anonymous rescue worker,** in a call to Rhode Island police

**Jan. 16** Scientists reveal the discovery of the remnants of a Greek trading vessel that sank to the bottom of the Black Sea at least 2,300 years ago. Laden with amphorae—jars or vases used by the ancients for a variety of purposes—it is the **oldest shipwreck ever found** in that sea, once a crossroads of commerce.

**Jan. 22** Chinese paleontologists report they have unearthed fossils of a four-winged **flying dinosaur** that last lived some 128 million years ago. Hailed as a "phenomenal find," the remains suggest, significantly, that birds glided before they developed true flight skills.

**Jan. 25** The largest U.S. exhibit of **Inca treasures** opens its national tour at Yale's Peabody Museum of Natural History. On display are hundreds of artifacts and a scale replica of the fabled Machu Picchu.

## The Stuff of Nightmares

It was morning on February 24 in Xinjiang, a region in China's remote northwest. In this land of terrible poverty, where people make about $72 a year, an earthquake with a 6.8 magnitude suddenly wrenched the ground beneath them as they ate their simple breakfasts. In the end, 268 lives were lost, and 18,000 houses were badly damaged or destroyed. These figures would have been still worse if the area were not so sparsely populated. Here, in Qiongkuerqiake, at the epicenter of the event, villagers prepare for bed in the freezing night air. Within days, blizzards would arrive, severely hampering rescue operations. Local officials vowed to rebuild the flattened homes within six months.

**Photograph by Goh Chai Hin** AFP

**❝ Lots of people are outside now and no one dares to stay at home. ❞**

— **Zhou Mincheng**, Flour mill operator

**Jan. 26** In their first **Super Bowl** triumph, the Tampa Bay Buccaneers defeat the favored Oakland Raiders, 48–21, in San Diego. Tampa Bay defensive back Dexter Jackson has two interceptions and is named Most Valuable Player.

**Feb. 1** Sixteen minutes before landing, the space shuttle *Columbia*, with a crew of seven aboard, stuns the world when it **disintegrates** nearly 40 miles above Earth.

**Feb. 13** Clara Harris, the 45-year-old dentist who ran over **her cheating husband** in a parking lot with her Mercedes, is found guilty of murder by a Texas jury. The mother of four-year-old twins, who has become a national cause célèbre, is later sentenced to 20 years.

## Trouble Brewing

In 1995 much of the Caribbean island of Montserrat was devastated when a volcano rocked the British holding. Two thirds of the population left, never to return. Then, two years later, all hell broke loose once more when another eruption buried much of southern Montserrat under gray ash. Here, in February, the Soufrière Hills volcano is summoning its forces yet again, readying to rain down its fury on the little country. All across the once bustling island, people are watching, waiting, dreading the worst. In the end, they have ample reason for fear. In the summer, the volcano suffers its largest dome collapse ever, and the entire land is smothered in heavy ash.

**Photograph by Stephen O'Meara**

**Feb. 14** Dolly, the world's **first cloned sheep,** is put down at age six after developing a progressive lung disease. Sheep commonly live to be twice that age.

**Feb. 15** Hundreds of thousands around the world **take to the streets** in a weekend of stormy demonstrations against the Allies' impending war with Iraq.

**Feb. 16** In **the biggest heist** in Antwerp's history, thieves break into 123 vaults in the Diamond Center and skedaddle with $100 million worth of jewels and gold. The Belgian city is the gem-trading capital of the world. Four suspects are arrested.

**Feb. 17** Blasting in from the Midwest, a **deadly blizzard** pummels the Northeast, burying Washington, D.C., New York and New England in up to two feet of snow while shutting down airports and stranding travelers. Dozens of lives are lost to the historic storm.

## Combating a Plague

Estimates from the United Nations put the number of AIDS sufferers at more than 40 million (25.3 million of them in sub-Saharan Africa), and say 21.8 million have died in the scourge, a fifth of them children under 15. (By way of contrast, the bubonic plague, history's worst health disaster, killed more than 25 million in the Middle Ages.) In Africa, more than 12 million children have been orphaned by AIDS. In February in Busia, Kenya, the Doctors Without Borders organization shows children a cartoon about AIDS prevention. For many of the kids, who live in mud huts, it is their first experience ever of TV.

**Photograph by Jake Price** SIPA Press

**❝ The teacher calls us orphans. But I don't want that name. Even other children don't want that name. ❞**

—**Kevina,** 14-year-old Ugandan girl who lost her parents, aunts and uncles to AIDS

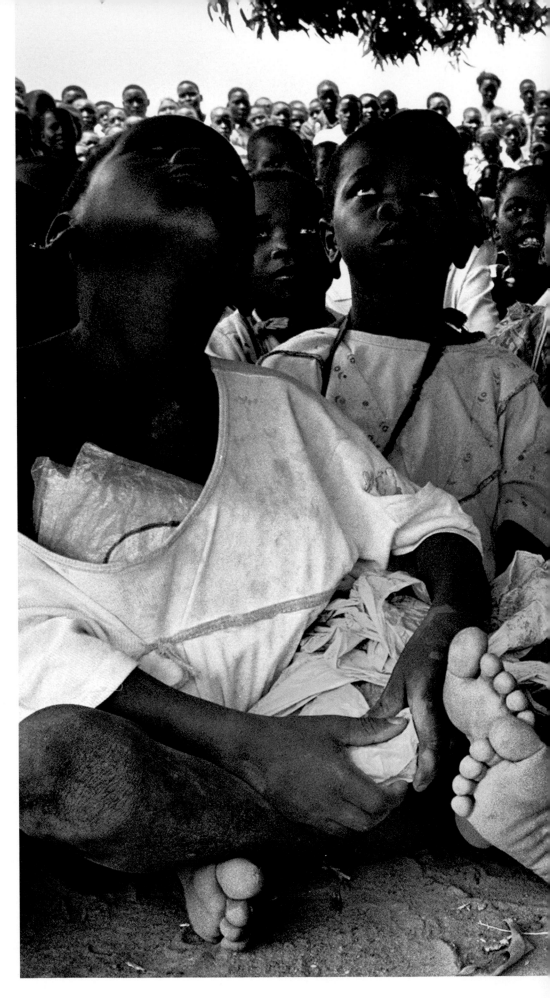

**Feb. 18** A South Korean **sets fire to a subway train** in Daegu, killing 198 people and injuring 147. Trapped passengers make desperate, last-minute cell-phone calls before smoke and flames engulf them. The mentally ill man, who was trying to kill himself but did not want to die alone, is later sentenced to life in prison.

**Feb. 22** Jesica Santillan, a 17-year-old Mexican immigrant, dies in the renowned Duke University Hospital two weeks after an unlikely episode in which she received heart and lungs **transplants that did not match** her blood type.

## Guns and Roses

It is, historically, a moot point whether mascara is mightier than the sword, but in an attempt to entice more women into the Russian army, there was a contest held in March called "Beauty in Epaulets." Here, two of the 16 finalists groom their Kalashnikovs as they prepare to demonstrate their skills as marksmen, the first of four competitions, held outside Moscow. The others were singing, ballroom dancing and cooking. When asked what the culinary contest would involve, an official replied, "Something like a salad." How successful these talented female soldiers will be at increasing their ranks remained to be seen, but to one male soldier present at the event, it didn't matter. "It's not women's work," said Vladimir.

**Photograph from AP**

**Feb. 24** John McMorran, **America's oldest man,** dies of heart failure in Lakeland, Fla., at age 113. For much of his life, said one family member, "he smoked cigars, drank beer and ate greasy food."

**March 1** A top bin Laden lieutenant and suspected **architect of the September 11 attacks,** Khalid Shaikh Mohammed, a.k.a. The Brain, is arrested in Pakistan.

**March 5** The U.S. Supreme Court votes 5–4 to uphold California's controversial **"three strikes" law,** which calls for mandatory terms of 25 years to life for felons convicted for the third time.

**March 11** Angered by a plan to raise the price of fertilizer, members of India's lower house of parliament employ their version of a filibuster—**screaming nonstop at the top of their lungs.** Four hours after the protest begins, the proposal is dropped.

# No Way Out?

In a long series of bad years for the Israeli-Palestinian conflict, 2003 was one of the worst. Israel considered Yasir Arafat persona non grata, and threatened to expel him from the region—or even perhaps kill him. Arafat, for his part, ended a power play with a puppet Palestinian prime minister by replacing him with a different puppet. For its part, the United States seemed to applaud one side, and then the other. Meanwhile, hundreds of people died in suicide bombings and military raids. On March 7, in the Gaza Strip, an Israeli armored vehicle and a dozen Palestinian boys are caught in the same photographic frame, providing an emblematic image of what has come before . . . and will come again.

**Photograph by Mohammed Saber** AFP

**March 19** "Let's go," says President George W. Bush, therein ordering the onset of **Operation Iraqi Freedom.**

**March 23** Army Pfc. Jessica Lynch, 19, of Palestine, W.Va., barely survives a firefight but is captured and taken to a hospital in Nasiriya. Rescued on April 1, she returns to the U.S. to **a hero's welcome.**

**March 23** *Chicago,* the first musical to win **Best Film** in 35 years, snares six Oscars on a night somewhat straitened by the war.

**March 27** The sky over four states in the Midwest is emblazoned with an **eerie blue light** after a meteor collides with the earth's atmosphere and scatters rocks the size of softballs in suburban Chicago.

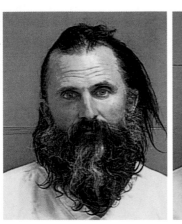

# An Ordeal Ends

On June 5, 2002, 14-year-old Elizabeth Smart was abducted from the family home in a well-to-do section of Salt Lake City. When a frantic manhunt proved fruitless over weeks and months, despair turned to abject sorrow, and few held out hope for her safe return. But on March 12, 2003, in the suburb of Sandy, 15 miles south of the city, Elizabeth was found in the company of Brian David Mitchell, 49, and his wife, Wanda Barzee, 57, who are charged with aggravated kidnapping, aggravated sexual assault and aggravated burglary. Elizabeth, a high school freshman, wrote in a book that her parents published in October: "Dear World: I am so happy and thankful to be home with the people I love. I'm doing great."

**Photograph by Francisco Kjolseth**
Salt Lake Tribune

**❝ The sky's just a little bit brighter in Utah today. ❞**

—**Chip Burris,** FBI agent

**March 30** "This is . . . the oldest evidence of mummification in Egypt," says the country's antiquities chief after a **5,000-year-old cedar coffin** is found near Cairo containing bones covered with the resin used in the ancient funerary process.

# FOCUS ON | "Columbia"

The space shuttle program—indeed, the entire notion of manned space efforts—had slipped from the national consciousness. And then tragedy snapped us awake.

Matt Stroshane/Getty Images

NASA

**In Outward Appearance, All Is A-O.K.**

Fifteen years of smooth sailing, and 87 missions since the shocking explosion of the space shuttle *Challenger,* had lulled the public into complacency about the manned space program. So when the orbiter *Columbia* lifted off on January 16 from Florida's Cape Canaveral, few noticed. Aboard were, clockwise from left, Kalpana Chawla, Dave Brown, Willie McCool, Michael Anderson, Ilan Ramon, Laurel Clark and Rick Husband.

Dr. Scott Lieberman/AP

Bill Ingalls/NASA

Steve Liss/Corbis

### "The *Columbia* Is Lost"

All that America knew was the two-week mission had proceeded smoothly. Later, it would learn that questions had been raised at NASA about liftoff problems that might have harmed *Columbia*. Affairs came to a dreadful conclusion on February 1 in the skies above Tyler, Tex., where debris was visible as *Columbia* disintegrated. Parts, including a helmet, pieces of the fuselage and a large, round tank of propellant, fell upon Nacogdoches and other rural outposts. NASA execs gathered in Washington, D.C., to contemplate the sadness of the day. The rest of the year was hardly more heartening for the space program. President Bush said at a memorial for the

crew, "This cause of exploration and discovery is not an option we choose. It is a desire written in the human heart," and in December there was even talk about resumed lunar exploration. But actions—as opposed to words—indicated that the road back to manned U.S. missions would be rocky indeed. After investigators chastised NASA, the agency's entire

nine-member board resigned. Even as American astronauts returned from the International Space Station and China became the third nation to launch a human being into space, Congress let it be known that all space appropriations requests would undergo intense scrutiny. The *Columbia*'s legacy therefore remained, at year's end, unwritten.

# Norah Jones

She seems so exotic, so sophisticated—with her background, looks and brand of music only underscoring the image—that people assume she is other than what she is: a shy, pleasant 24-year-old woman from Grapevine, Texas.

For the longest time, her life was very quiet. There were the growing-up years, with her single mom in the suburbs of Dallas, and the many lonely hours of piano practice. Even after she went to New York City, the scenes were still quiet. As recently as three years ago, Norah Jones was playing at a suitably named club, the Living Room, situated on Manhattan's Lower East Side. Or she was at Makor, the hangout for young singles at the Jewish Community Center on West 67th. She joined a couple of bands—the Ferdinandos, Wax Poetic—that didn't do much, but this was O.K. too because she liked her bandmates a lot. Jesse Harris wrote some terrific songs, Norah thought, and she particularly took to the bass player, Lee Alexander, who became her boyfriend. Jones moved out of the Living Room and into Joe's Pub over in the Village, and word started to get around. By now, a demo tape had landed her a deal at Blue Note Records, the jazz record label, and she started to sketch her album. Jesse wrote some new songs, Norah dusted off some of Mom's favorite tunes and a Hank Williams chestnut, and on February 26, 2002, a CD called *Come Away with Me* was released. Everything was still very quiet in the world of Norah Jones.

Eleven months later, the disc, after a strong and steady climb, reached No. 1 on the *Billboard* charts—an altogether astonishing performance for a collection of serene, soulful songs. When a million copies had been sold, Jones panicked and asked her record company to stop selling it. They smiled and politely declined, and *Come Away with Me* went double platinum, triple, quadruple . . . until more than 10 million copies had been sold. In February

**Music came naturally: Jones's father is Ravi Shankar, the Indian sitarist who mentored the Beatles in the 1960s and who had a nine-year relationship with Sue Jones, then a concert promoter in New York City. After Shankar left, Sue took young Norah to Texas.**

came Jones's coronation at the Grammy Awards: five wins, including Album of the Year over Bruce Springsteen's hugely favored *The Rising,* plus three more for the CD's production and for Harris's ballad "Don't Know Why" as Song of the Year.

"I wanna see an end to this record, and all of this other stuff," Jones told *Rolling Stone,* while admitting that she was tickled by the acclaim. "More people have heard my album than I've ever dreamed of, so it's like, 'Whoa! Stop the presses! We're cool. Dude, that's enough.'"

The presses will soon roll again, as Jones has returned to the studio (left) to record her follow-up CD. While it can never be the miracle that was *Come Away with Me,* there is every chance that it, too, will be cool. Dude.

# Spring

## A Young Man's Fancy

For many, spring begins with a day on the calendar. For some it is the first robin or the opening of the fishing season. But for lots of others, spring arrives with the playing of the Masters in Augusta, Ga., with azaleas and honeysuckle bringing promise of gentler days. For Mike Weir, playing this approach shot to the 13th green means that he is a couple of dozen swings away from winning his first major championship, in a tournament known for drama. This year, there was tension off the links as well. Augusta National is for men only, and many women, activist Martha Burk in particular, deemed that unacceptable. Club chairman Hootie Johnson refused to budge, however, and while picketers held forth a ways down the road, the gents once more called the shots in Augusta.

**Photograph by David Cannon/Getty**

## Solemn and Celebratory

Holy Week in the heavily Catholic Andalusian region of southern Spain means different things to different people, but it is uniformly marked by intensity and passion. In the capital of Seville it is, on Holy Thursday and Good Friday, a reverent time; women dress in black, and T-shirted tourists are seen as disrespectful. But then, throughout the week, there are scores of daily parades, as floats snake through city streets. These festivities are followed by all-night-long carousing in the cafes. Here, on the Wednesday between Palm Sunday and Easter, penitents young and older affiliated with El Baratillo, one of the religious brotherhoods in Seville, make their way to the start of the day's procession.

**Photograph by Marcelo del Pozo** Reuters

**April 1** For a second time in as many weeks, a plane from Cuba is forced to land on Key West. The hijacker, packing **dummy grenades,** surrenders, and all passengers and crew—among them the man's wife and three-year-old child—are unharmed.

**April 14** In a surprise announcement, **biological code-crackers** report that they have finished sequencing the human genetic map—three billion units of DNA— two years ahead of schedule. They describe their accomplishment as "the instruction set that carries each of us from the one-cell egg . . . to the grave."

**April 16** "This is the final retirement," says **basketball wizard** Michael Jordan, 40, after scoring the final 15 points of his career in a game against the Philadelphia 76ers. This is his third "retirement."

**April 18** Scott Peterson is arrested in San Diego after DNA tests identify the bodies of Laci, **his 27-year-old pregnant wife,** and her unborn baby boy. Late in the year, a judge orders him to stand trial. Laci had vanished on Christmas Eve in 2002.

## Cause for Concern

In late 2002, people in China's Guangdong province began to fall ill to a mysterious disease. Some cases proved fatal. In February 2003 a man from there, who had the symptoms and would later become known as Patient A, checked into a hotel in Hong Kong. Thus the disease known as SARS (severe acute respiratory syndrome) was passed on to travelers from Singapore, Ireland, Germany and Canada. Fears of a global pandemic on the order of AIDS spread rapidly. But in July, after 8,098 cases in 32 countries, after 744 deaths, the crisis passed. Here, in Hong Kong, ballet lessons proceed on April 27.

**Photograph by Vincent Yu** AP

**❝ We are keeping an open mind. ❞**

—**Dr. Julie L. Gerberding,** director of the Centers for Disease Control and Prevention, when asked in March if the mystery illness might be bioterrorism, a concept that is later deemed unlikely

**April 22** Hundreds of nervous patrons rush to a bank in New York City's Chinatown to withdraw their money following **rumors of impropriety** by a bank manager. A similar panic ensues at a Philadelphia branch the next day.

**April 27** After **arsenic-laced coffee** is served during a social hour at a Lutheran church in New Sweden, Maine, 16 parishioners are poisoned, one of them fatally. Police link a later suicide to the case, but continue to investigate, suspecting the existence of an accomplice.

**April 29** A **2.5-ton satellite** reenters Earth's atmosphere and splashes harmlessly into the Pacific Ocean—a relief to people in 39 countries who had been alerted they might be targets of debris.

## A Deep Thirst

Here, in the western Indian state of Gujarat, the worst drought in a century has ravaged the land for five years. These people have gathered in sweltering temperatures to get water from a large well; otherwise they must wait for hours for state-run water tankers to show up in their villages. What's worse, Gujarat, with its population in excess of 40 million, was just one of nine states afflicted by the drought. The good news is that rainfall in coming weeks would help matters, at least for the time being.

**Photograph by Amit Dave** Reuters

**May 1** In a **photo-op** of presidential proportions, George W. Bush lands on the USS *Abraham Lincoln* in a Navy Viking jet, then strides across the deck in a flight suit. With a MISSION ACCOMPLISHED banner as a backdrop, he tells cheering sailors, "Major combat operations in Iraq have ended."

**May 1** Jayson Blair, a 27-year-old reporter for *The New York Times,* is forced to resign after it is learned that he **plagiarized** or simply made up dozens of stories. A month later, two of the tarnished paper's top editors quit under pressure.

**May 5** "My gambling days are over," says Bill Bennett, author of *The Book of Virtues,* after it is reported that the **self-styled moralist** has lost some $8 million playing video poker and the slot machines at casinos in Atlantic City and Las Vegas.

**May 8** At 33,000 feet above eastern Congo, the rear door of a Russian-built Ilyushin 76 cargo plane bursts open and dozens of passengers are **sucked out through the plane's gaping hole.**

## Soaring

In 1968, on the grounds of her Maryland home, Eunice Kennedy Shriver sought to help children with learning disabilities by organizing games and contests for them. Thus began the Special Olympics, which long ago spread coast to coast and now is a global phenomenon with 1.2 million participants, a 22 percent increase since 2000. In June, the Special Olympics World Summer Games were held outside the U.S. for the first time ever, fittingly in Shriver's ancestral homeland, Ireland. Some 7,000 athletes in 166 delegations took part in 21 sports, constituting the largest sporting event in the world in 2003. On June 23, Great Britain's Emma Stokes nails her balance beam routine.

**Photograph by Steve Humphreys** EPA

**May 14** Eighteen illegal aliens die after being trapped inside a **sweltering tractor-trailer** driving in southeastern Texas. A few of the hundred-some Mexican and Central American immigrants had poked out the tail lights to get help—and air.

**May 24** Known as "Money" to his friends, Chris Moneymaker lays down $40 and turns it into $2.5 million at the 2003 **World Series of Poker** in Las Vegas. The champ, a 27-year-old accountant from Spring Hill, Ten., is the first person to win the tournament by qualifying on the Internet.

**May 31** On the FBI's Most Wanted list for five years, Eric Rudolph is arrested by an alert policeman who discovers him scavenging for food in a Murphy, N.C., Dumpster. The 36-year-old fugitive is the prime suspect for the **bombing at the 1996 Atlanta Olympics,** as well as several other blasts.

## Street Fighting Boy

Located in West Africa, Liberia was founded in the 19th century by freed American slaves, whose descendants now make up 5 percent of the population. Things were essentially calm until the 1980s; late in the decade a man named Charles Taylor entered a scene of intense upheaval. Taylor launched a campaign that turned on ethnic conflicts, and used his army of children—they called him Pappy—to finally take over. He was elected president in 1997. His tenure was characterized by brutality and murder (since 1989 there have been 200,000 deaths in the troubled state). In June he was ensconced in the capital city of Monrovia, where terror reigned until international pressures drove him into exile.

**Photograph by George Gobet** AFP

**❝ He killed my Ma, he killed my Pa, but I will vote for him. ❞**

—A campaign slogan for Taylor

**June 3** Chicago Cubs slugger Sammy Sosa is ejected in a game against the Tampa Bay Devil Rays after he is caught using a **corked bat.** "I use that bat for batting practice," he claims. Although a search reveals no other illegal bats, Sosa is suspended from play for seven games.

**June 4** "The journey we're taking is difficult but **there is no other choice,**" says President Bush after a meeting in Aqaba, Jordan, with Palestinian Prime Minister Mahmoud Abbas and Israeli Prime Minister Ariel Sharon. Just over a week later, new violence erupts in the Middle East, upsetting "the road map to peace." Three months later, Abbas resigns.

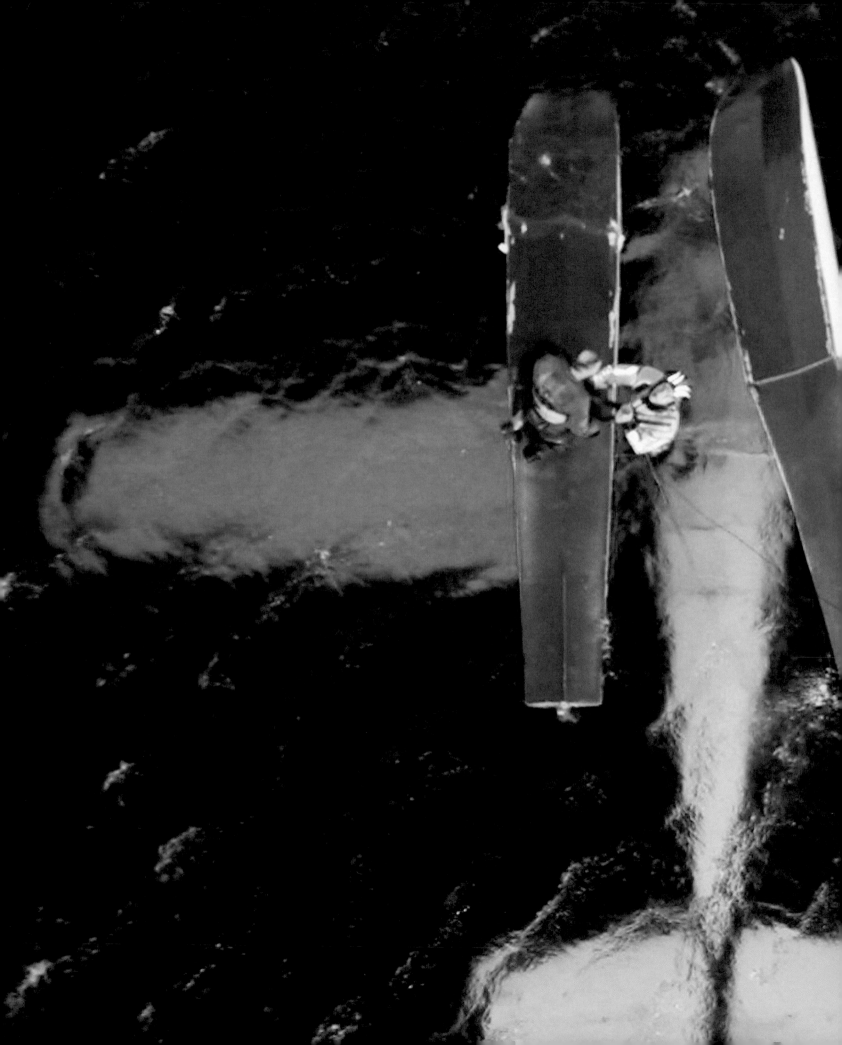

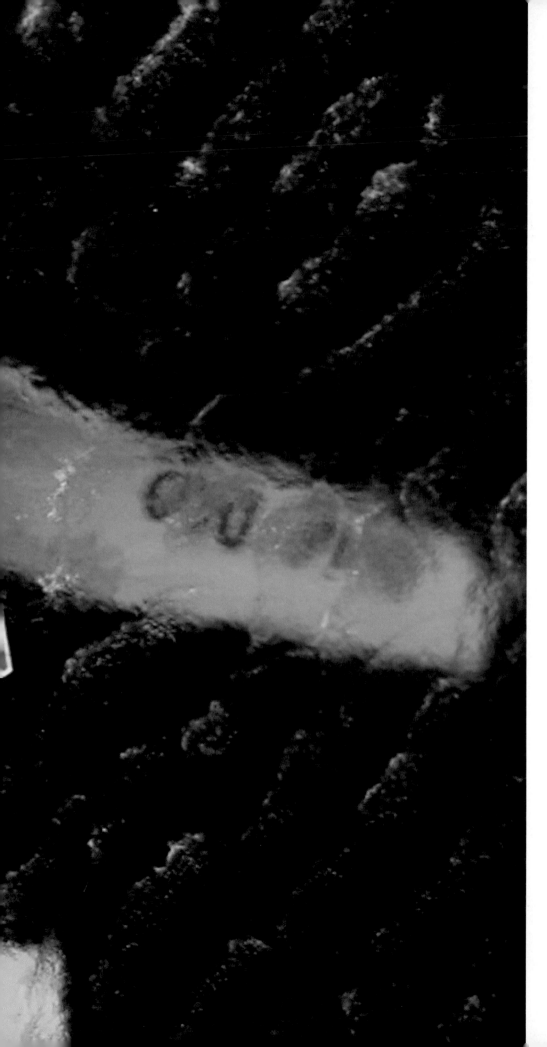

## Bottom's Up

Ole Julius Eriksen is a familiar name in far northern Norway. The bush pilot has been picking people up and plunking them down on or near remote lakes in Finnmark County since the 1960s. Late on June 30, Eriksen prepared to take off in his seaplane from the surface of Lessjavri Lake with a very important passenger aboard, his six-year-old boy. Rumbling across the surface, the scene lit by the midnight sun, the seaplane struck a rock and flipped over. Father and son scrambled from the cockpit as people on shore, who had seen the mishap, phoned for help. A helicopter from the nearby Banak rescue station arrived within minutes and plucked the Eriksens from the cold water. All that was bruised was the old bush pilot's legend.

**Photograph from EPA/AP**

**June 4** Martha Stewart says she is innocent after she is indicted for obstructing justice on allegations of **insider trading.** She later resigns as chairman and chief executive officer of Martha Stewart Living Omnimedia.

**June 11** Paleontologists in Africa report the discovery of **160,000-year-old skulls** of two adults and a child, perhaps the oldest remains of Homo sapiens. The scientists say this is further proof that man originated in Africa.

**June 21** At midnight, *Harry Potter and the Order of the Phoenix,* the fifth installment in the popular series, goes on sale. By the end of the day, an estimated **five million copies** of the books have been sold. More than one fifth of them had been preordered on Amazon.

**June 23** Voting 5 to 4, the U.S. Supreme Court preserves **affirmative action** in university admissions, but in another decision bans a system in which extra points are granted to minorities.

# FOCUS ON The War in Iraq

Was Iraq a threat to global stability? Was it a haven for terrorists? The questions loomed as the conflict was joined. And they would persist—even with the capture of Saddam.

**Target: Baghdad**
By the time bombs fall on the Iraqi capital on March 21, the U.S. has made clear to the world that its goal is complete victory and regime change. In 1990, when Saddam Hussein defied the world and invaded Kuwait, U.S. President George Bush swiftly assembled a coalition. Operation Desert Storm pushed Iraq back, but did not push on to Baghdad, or topple Hussein. The campaign ordered in 2003 by President George W. Bush would be different.

Mirrorpix/Getty

Sergio Barrenechea/EFE/Sipa

Harry Cubluck/AP

Andrew Parsons/PA/ABACA

## Debate, Dissent, Decisions

On February 22, 2001, the U.S. bombed Iraqi missile sites. The new President Bush said the goal was to send Saddam "a clear message." For the next two years, a countdown to war continued, as Bush alternately linked Hussein to terrorists (perhaps including those behind September 11), accused him of stockpiling weapons of mass destruction, and pushed for United Nations resolutions against Iraq. Finally, in mid-2002 and early '03, the U.S. began talking of formal warfare. With dissent at home and huge protests abroad (left, London on February 15), Bush struggled to build a coalition like his father's. Above: On March 16, Great Britain's Tony Blair and Spain's Jose Maria Aznar pledge allegiance, but absent are leaders from France and Germany, which oppose the war. Right: In March, Spc. Michael Tanner hugs his family before he and others of the 4th Infantry are deployed from Fort Hood, Tex.

## On the Ground

After the first bombs fell, Coalition troops entered Iraq from the south. In the first week of the war, despite "Shock and Awe" bombing of Baghdad and the quick taking of the southern city of Basra, progress was generally difficult, and in places there was confusion—Is Saddam dead?—and even chaos. Above: On March 21, a British Royal Marine fires a wire-guided missile at an Iraqi position on the Al Faw peninsula. Right: On March 25, Iraqis race to pick up rations thrown from a U.S. convoy near the southern city of Nasiriya.

### The Slog of War

Further complicating matters, on March 25 a sandstorm of historic proportions engulfed Iraq. Here, troops from the U.S. 1st Marine Division shield their eyes as their truck stops on the road from Nasiriya to Baghdad. The next day, Marines head north, passing a dead Iraqi soldier.

### Casualties of Many Kinds

There were others besides soldiers and civilians who were in harm's way. The Pentagon, reacting to criticism of its media blackout of Gulf War I, decided to allow 600 "embedded" journalists to travel with the Coalition troops; other daring freelancers made their way into the country as well. Fourteen died during the month of "official" war—including NBC correspondent David Bloom, who above is being removed from the field on April 6— and there were additional casualties among journalists afterward. Left: Army Pfc. Jessica Lynch, who barely survived a March 23 firefight and was wounded badly, is rescued from an Iraqi hospital a week later by American Special Forces. Right: On March 29, a U.S. Marine medic near Rifa, in eastern Iraq, cradles a four-year-old girl. Her mother had been killed in a frontline cross fire, U.S. officials said.

Scott Nelson/Getty

Kuni Takahashi/Boston Herald/ReflexNews

### Closing In

During the third week of the war, sand- and rainstorms behind them, Coalition forces gained momentum and were racing toward Baghdad. Above: On April 4, the VIP terminal of Saddam International Airport is host to soldiers from the 3rd Infantry, who move from room to room during a dawn advance on Iraq's capital. Left: On April 7, members of the 3rd Battalion, 4th Marine Regiment exhort their comrades across the Diyala Bridge, just southeast of Baghdad. The bridge wasn't strong enough to support tanks, so it had to be taken by foot. Two Marines were killed.

Goran Tomasevic/Reuters

## Saddam Has Fallen, but Has He Been Killed?

On April 4, even as the Coalition's victory is a certainty to the wider world, Saddam is seen on Iraqi TV rallying supporters. (But is it Saddam? Is it a double?) To the end, the regime insisted that it would prevail: "The infidels are committing suicide by the hundreds on the gates of Baghdad . . . As our leader Saddam Hussein said, 'God is grilling their stomachs in hell.'" But when U.S. forces entered the city, the opposition had fled. Below, on April 9, a soldier stands guard in Firdos Square as Iraqis and Marines pull down a statue of Saddam. Subsequently, Iraqis stomped on the statue, then rode its detached head through the streets. Still later, tapes of Saddam began surfacing, taunting U.S. authorities, who admitted that, once more, he may have survived.

**A City Turned Upside Down**

In the week after Baghdad's fall, scenes ranging from the joyous to the tragic to the positively surreal were acted out. Here, on April 16, Gen. Tommy Franks holds a news conference in one of Saddam's former palaces, which are now in Coalition hands and being used as headquarters, prisons and sites for photo ops. Franks, the four-star general who directed the invasion, had flown into the newly named Baghdad International Airport for a progress report, to meet with commanders in the field and to begin planning Iraq's reconstruction. Two days earlier, American forces had overrun Tikrit, the city near Saddam's ancestral home and the assumed last bastion of his support. And then the President, acting on advisories from his generals, said confidently: "The regime of Saddam Hussein is no more."

## Running Wild in the Streets

Although looting in a postwar environment is as old as war itself, the repeated images of thievery and the pilfering of ancient artifacts made this war's plundering seem somehow more decadent. Further, the rampant lawlessness came to symbolize the concerns of many that the Coalition had launched its war without having a solid postwar plan. Above: On April 11, two women carry furniture away from a government office building that is on fire in downtown Baghdad. On April 13, National Museum Deputy Director Mushin Hasan holds his head in his hands as he sits amidst destroyed artifacts. Coalition soldiers swooped in to help, but too late.

Antonin Kratochvil/VII

Dario Mitidieri

### Coming to Terms with an Awful Past

Even before the war, it was no secret that Iraq's majority Shiite population and the minority Kurdish people of the north had been persecuted to the point of genocide by Saddam's Sunni Muslim regime. Now the evidence was unearthed, as mass graves were found near Baghdad, Najaf, Basra, Tharthar and, above, Karbala, where several thousand corpses were discovered. Few mourned when Saddam's murderous sons Uday (below, right) and Qusai were killed in late July in a gun battle in Mosul.

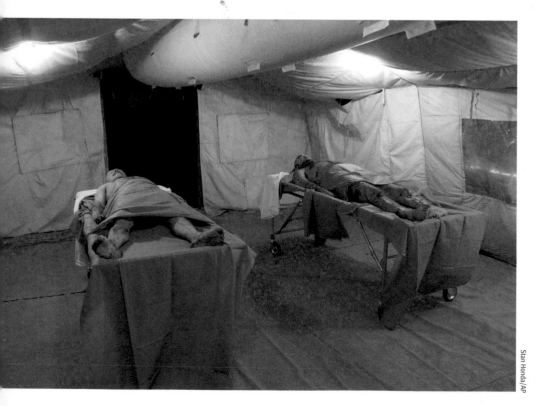

Stan Honda/AP

## Coming to Terms with a Dangerous Present

President Bush could declare, as he had on May 1 while wearing a flight suit and speaking to servicemen aboard the USS *Abraham Lincoln,* that major fighting was over. But the reality in Iraq seemed otherwise. There were constant bomb threats in schools, living quarters for Coalition peacekeepers were shot at, and suicide bombings became regular occurrences: In late October, five of them in 30 hours killed at least 40 and wounded more than 225. Tuesday, October 28, was a pivotal day: Two U.S. soldiers were killed when their Abrams tank hit a mine 50 miles north of Baghdad, and with that, more American troops—117—had been killed in combat during the occupation than during the conflict. Above: On July 5, U.S. National Guardsmen go house to house in Baghdad searching for weapons.

Robert Schmidt/AFP

## The Insurgency Continues

The enemy were called guerrillas now rather than soldiers, but the havoc they wreaked was more horrific than any caused by Saddam's army. Surface-to-air fire downed helicopters: one near Tikrit on October 25, two more during the first week of November, killing 22 in all. A week later, a Black Hawk avoiding gunfire crashed into a second copter over Mosul; 17 more died. Above: In Tikrit on October 16, soldiers mourn the death of Spc. Donald Laverne Wheeler Jr., killed in an attack on an armored vehicle. Right: the rubble of U.N. headquarters in Baghdad after a truck bomb killed 24.

Suhaib Salem/Reuters

## The Tyrant Is Captured

On December 13, having been betrayed by a member of his clan, a haggard, disoriented Saddam Hussein is found in a cramped "spider hole" at a farm outside Tikrit. He has a pistol but is taken without incident, as a U.S. soldier tells him, "President Bush sends his regards." Hussein insists he had no direct role in the insurgency. Perhaps in proof, 12 hours after he is taken, at least 17 police are killed by a bomb. On December 15, eleven insurgents are killed in a firefight north of Baghdad. A day later, a roadside bomb in Tikrit wounds three soldiers. The Ace of Spades is in hand, but the war is not yet over.

AP/U.S. Military via APTN

# Aron Ralston

Following his muse, a young man left the deskbound world to spend his life among the high, white peaks of Colorado. One day, deep in a Utah canyon, something went horribly wrong, and the young man faced his crucible.

Dan Bayer/Polaris

Aron Ralston/Polaris

**W**hen he had escaped the canyon and word began to circulate about what he had done, there was disbelief—first in Utah, where it happened, and then everywhere, at the dinner table, at the watercooler. How many days was he in there? When did his water run out? And then—*goodness*—he did what?

On April 26, Aron Ralston was a 27-year-old former Intel engineer who had relocated to Aspen, Colo., to become an outdoors guide. By the previous year he had knocked off several big peaks: the highest points in 34 states, including 20,320-foot Denali in Alaska. As he left his truck at a trailhead and mountain-biked 15 miles to the entrance of Bluejohn Canyon to begin a solo descent, he was a six-foot-two, fit, experienced mountaineer—who had neglected to tell

Dan Bayer/Polaris

Detective Greg Funk/Emery County Sheriff's Office

"At no point was I ever able to get the boulder to budge even microscopically," said Ralston. Within five months of his release from the hospital, he had climbed six of Colorado's 14,000-foot mountains and had been kayaking with the aid of a prosthetic forearm.

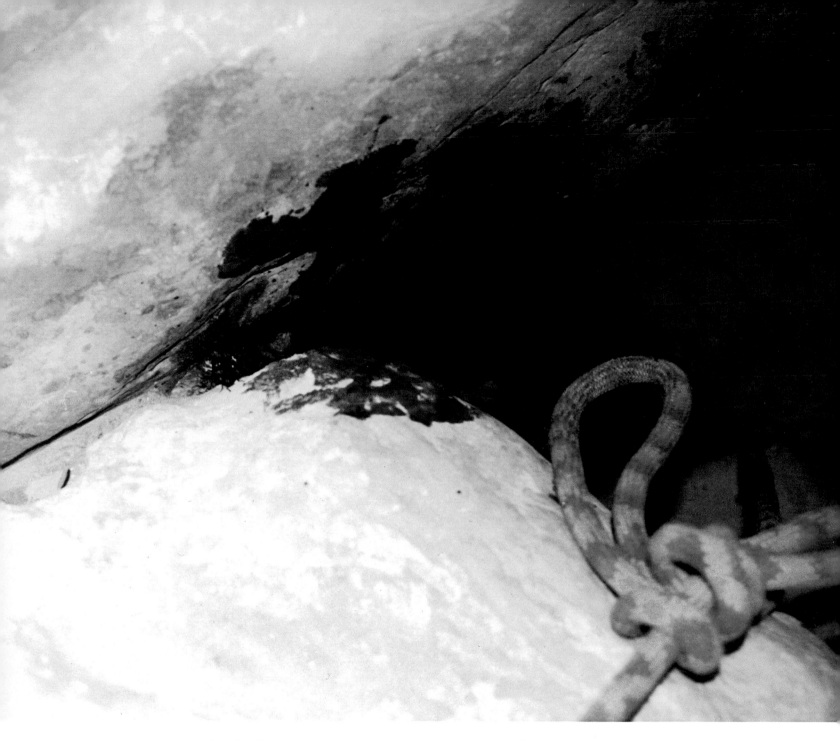

friends where he was going, "something I almost always do but I failed to do this time."

Ralston was maneuvering between two ledges when an 800-pound boulder came loose and crashed onto his right hand, trapping it against the sandstone wall. The pain was excruciating as he made futile efforts to get free. "The adrenaline was pumping very, very hard," he said later. "It took some good, calm thinking to get myself to calm down and stop throwing myself against the boulder." The next five days were spent going through meager rations (two burritos, a liter of water), trying to move the boulder with his climbing ropes,

suffering times of abject despair, then coming "to peace with death." Having lost 40 pounds, he saw, finally, only one solution. He used leverage to snap his arm bones above the wrist. He applied a tourniquet and, in an hour, amputated his hand and part of his arm with a dull blade. "I was so happy to be taking action," he said. "All the desires, joys and euphorias of a future life came rushing into me."

Liberated, he rappelled 66 feet to the floor of the canyon and struggled five miles downstream before meeting three other hikers. A helicopter that had been searching for him shuttled him to a Moab hospital, where Aron Ralston began his future life.

## Eye of the Monster

This image of Hurricane Isabel, captured by the International Space Station on September 15, shows the frightening storm heading for the eastern seaboard of the United States. At sea, Isabel reached Category 5, the highest level of hurricane intensity. In fact, when well offshore, winds measured above 210 mph. In the event, despite authorities taking every precaution—the federal government in Washington, D.C., was shut down for two days—there was widespread destruction and dozens of lives were lost.

**Photograph by NASA**

Summer

## So Close, yet Still So Far

In the summer, Mars was to draw as close to Earth as it had in 59,619 years. Yes, the proximity would still leave the red planet 34.65 million miles distant, but no matter—in the southern sky, the sphere would glow brighter than any other planet or star. Backyard astronomers and the pros behind the Hubble eagerly examined surface features through their telescopes, but a photographer from Long Beach, Calif., set himself a different mission. "I wanted to shoot Mars from a place that looked like Mars," said Wally Pacholka. "I made the 700-mile round trip to the incredibly scenic Valley of Fire State Park in Nevada six times." This image, with Poodle Rock in the extreme foreground, was his reward.

**Photograph by Wally Pacholka** AstroPics

**July 3** "This is the closest we have yet got to a real **solar system–like planet** . . . like our own," says one of the astronomers who found the sphere just 90 light-years away. Approximately twice the mass of Jupiter, the "new" planet orbits its sun, HD 70642, every six years.

**July 5** For her second **Wimbledon** title, Serena Williams defeats her older sister, Venus, who is hampered by injuries sustained earlier in the tournament. "I just had to tell myself to look at the ball and nothing else," Serena says after her bittersweet 4–6, 6–4, 6–2 victory. The next day, Roger Federer of Switzerland wins the men's singles match in straight sets.

**July 16** A Santa Monica open market becomes a scene of horror when an 86-year-old man plows his red 1992 Buick through a crowd of shoppers, **killing 10 and injuring 80.** "My heart is broken over the extent of the tragedy," says the remorseful driver.

## Field of Dreams

Nothing is as gay as a sunflower, but for this young German woman, helpless in a struggle with nature, their joy is but a memory. And she was not alone. Most of Europe fell prey to hellish temperatures that in the west alone killed more than 35,000 people. In France, fatalities numbered 14,802, igniting public complaints about the national health system that led to the resignation of their director general of health. Not even the pope's prayers on August 10 could bring any relief, as the heat and its concomitant drought withered the continent's economy as well.

**Photograph by Hermann Bredehorst**
Polaris

**" You have to take care of your elderly. "**
— **Dr. Bernard Kouchner,** former French health minister

**July 18** Dr. David Kelly, Britain's **top expert on biological weapons** and adviser to the Ministry of Defense, is found near his home after having slit his wrist. Three days prior to his suicide, he had testified at an inquiry into whether Tony Blair had exaggerated the extent of Iraq's weapons program.

**July 18** At a news conference in Eagle, Colo., prosecutors announce they will charge basketball star **Kobe Bryant,** 25, with sexually assaulting a 19-year-old hotel worker on June 30.

**July 22** Thick black smoke rising from an electrical fire envelops the top corner of **the Eiffel Tower** in the early evening. Thousands of visitors are forced to evacuate.

## A Ship's Tale

Built in 1853, the side-wheel steamer *Tennessee* was a commercial craft. Then, in January 1862, she was seized by the Confederates and may have been used for blockade running. In April, the Union side took *Tennessee* during the capture of New Orleans. The swift vessel was used for most of the rest of the Civil War for blockade, supply and dispatch duties in the Gulf of Mexico. In 1864, the North seized the former Confederate ironclad *Tennessee*— same name, different boat—so the older ship was renamed the *Mobile*. Near the end of the conflict, she was returned to commercial duties as the *Republic,* but in October 1865, carrying gold coins, she was lost in a storm off Savannah. This summer, a salvage firm located the ship; one expert said the coins could be worth $150 million to collectors. Here, the ship's bell lies as it was found.

**Photograph by Odyssey Marine Exploration**

**July 27** "This tour took a lot out of me," says Lance Armstrong, 31, after winning his fifth straight Tour de France, the **grueling 23-day bicycling competition.** Edging out Germany's Jan Ullrich by 61 seconds overall, Armstrong notches his narrowest victory, becoming only the second cyclist to win five straight Tours, and one of five to win five Tours in all.

**Aug. 6** Twice a week, Albert Lexie rises at five a.m., takes two buses to the Children's Hospital in Pittsburgh and gives $3 shoe-shines. He earns $10,000 a year, yet since 1981 he has donated $89,000 to the hospital's Free Care Fund, which helps needy pediatric patients. On his 61st birthday, his friends give him a **shoe-shine kit on wheels** to accommodate the 30-pound box he has lugged on his back all these years.

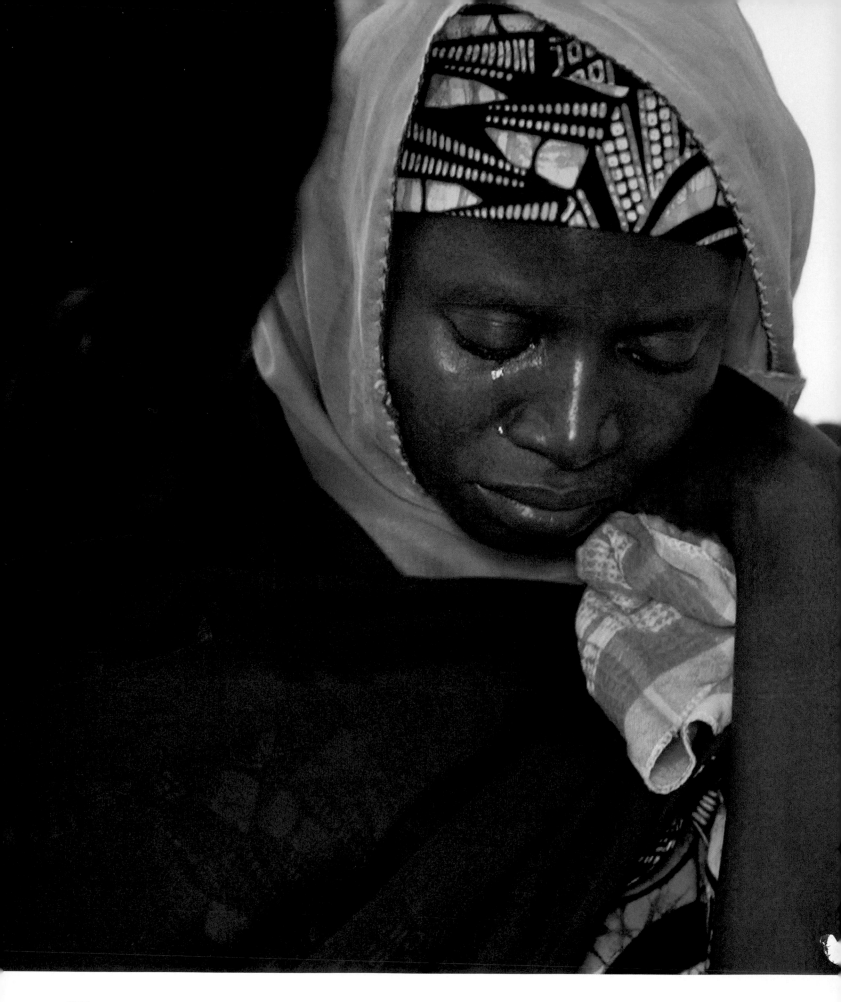

## Injustice Averted

After Amina Lawal, a 30-year-old Muslim woman in northern Nigeria, was sentenced in March 2002 to death by stoning for bearing a child out of wedlock, an international uproar ensued; Amnesty International was among the many to enter the fray. The outcry against this verdict under stern Islamic Shariah law, which is practiced in 12 of Nigeria's 36 states, factored into granting Lawal an appeal. On August 27, 2003, Lawal brings her child, Wasila, to the courtroom in Katsina, and sheds a tear before her argument is to be heard. A month later she is "hereby discharged and acquitted." While technicalities regarding her prosecution are cited by the court, no mention is made of reforming Shariah law or removing stoning as an available sentence.

**Photograph by Saurabh Das** AP

> **❝ I am happy . . . All I want is to go home, get married and live a normal life. ❞**
>
> —**Amina Lawal**

**Aug. 19** Members of the media watch the 100 millionth newly designed $20 bill come off the presses at the Bureau of Engraving and Printing's Western Currency Facility in Fort Worth. To combat ever more clever **counterfeiters,** certain denominations have to be redesigned every seven to 10 years. The new bill is the first U.S. currency in a century to feature colors—peach, light blue—other than green, black and white, and it will be issued on Oct. 9.

**Aug. 23** An inmate at a correctional facility in Shirley, Mass., **attacks and kills** a fellow inmate, defrocked Roman Catholic priest John Geoghan, 68, who had been convicted of child molestation in 2002.

## Woe Are the Worker Bees

When intermittent rain postponed play for a third straight day at the U.S. Open in New York on September 3, the tennis royals were talking about the weather—and not very nicely. "They spent more time drying the courts than it rained," said Queen Mum Martina Navratilova, still playing doubles at age 46. "Yesterday, it was two hours of play, six hours of drying." The kingly boo birds—Andre Agassi and Andy Roddick chief among them—wondered aloud why a tournament as rich as the Open didn't have at least some courts covered by a roof. Though Agassi got beat, Roddick settled down. Did he ever. On a hot Sunday, he won his first Grand Slam title at age 21, having never lost serve in the tournament.

**Photograph by Shaun Best** Reuters

**Aug. 25** NASA launches SIRTF (Space Infrared Telescope Facility), the last of the "Great Observatories," at Cape Canaveral. Astronomer William Waller says the powerful instrument "will peer into places **no telescope has ever seen,** sensing the infrared sky with unsurpassed sensitivity."

**Aug. 25** Activists belonging to a radical animal-rights group **liberate 10,000 minks** from a fur farm near Seattle. Volunteers with snares and nets try to rescue them, but late in the year, some of the wily creatures are still running free.

**Aug. 27** A five-man moving crew hoists a 5,280-pound **granite carving of the Ten Commandments** from the rotunda of Alabama's Supreme Court in Montgomery. Installed by Chief Justice Roy Moore one night in 2001, the religious artifact was deemed inappropriate by a federal court. He is removed from office on November 13 but tells his supporters, "The battle is not over. The battle to acknowledge God is about to rage across the country."

## Now You See Him . . .

A few years ago, David Blaine began to make a national name for himself as a "street magician." TV cameras followed him as he prowled urban avenues, performing his sleight-of-hand wizardry for passersby who howled with disbelief, all the while punctuated by Blaine's nasal semipunk palaver. Here, next to London's Tower Bridge on September 6, he begins a 44-day stint in a sealed plastic box suspended 40 feet high with no food, only water. "Blaine baiting" became a national pastime; madcap Britons delighted in teasing Blaine with insults and food temptations. Well, in the end he made it, but only he knows how—or why. To advocates for hunger victims, Blaine's act appeared grossly insensitive.

**Photograph by Sion Touhig** Polaris

> **" I will have to endure by adapting and surviving as an animal would. On instinct. "**
>
> — **David Blaine**

**Aug. 30** Three years after the sinking of the *Kursk,* a Russian nuclear sub, another one goes down in the Barents Sea. This time it is a 40-year-old decommissioned craft. Nine of the *K-159*'s crew are lost, a fraction of the 118 who died on the *Kursk.* But the threat of **leaking radioactive material** is far greater because of *K-159*'s age and corroded hull.

**Sept. 10** While shopping in a department store in Stockholm, Anna Lindh, 46, **Sweden's charismatic foreign minister** and an ardent campaigner for adopting the euro, is stabbed in the arms, chest and stomach by an unidentified man. After more than 10 hours of surgery, the mother of two dies the next day. Three days later, despite a surge of sympathy, Swedes vote against adopting the euro.

## The Word on The Street

Two different men enjoyed—or didn't—very different years on Wall Street. Their fortunes took crucial turns in September. New York State Attorney General Eliot Spitzer (left), who had already made conflict-of-interest issues in brokerage firms a big deal, was happy to appear at financial summits with New York Stock Exchange chief Richard Grasso early in '03, when this photo was taken. But shortly thereafter, Spitzer questioned Grasso's own possible conflicts in sitting on the boards of Exchange members. Grasso then came under fire for the huge pay package—seven score million and more—he was due for boosting the Exchange in the eyes of investors. Grasso resigned under pressure on September 17, even as Spitzer was pushing his newest crusade: criminal cases against mutual funds that may have favored mega-money investors over the little guy.

**Photograph by Stefan Zaklin** Getty

**Sept. 21** Lulu, a **partially blind eastern gray kangaroo,** pays back a debt and becomes a hero. After her mother was killed, she was adopted by Leonard Richards, 52, a farmer near Morwell, Australia. On this day, Lulu finds him lying in a field near his home. She barks "like a dog" and alerts his family, who discover Richards has been knocked unconscious by a falling branch. He recovers, and Lulu once more follows him around the farm, as she has done for 10 years.

**Sept. 22** The **youngest student ever** to attend the University of Chicago's Pritzker School of Medicine, Sho Yano, 12, gets his white doctor's coat in a ceremony to launch his studies to become a cancer geneticist. He also plays the piano and has a black belt in tae kwon do.

## A Wee Walk in the Loch

Lloyd Scott, a 41-year-old former fire-fighter and professional soccer player, is standing on the shore of Scotland's storied Loch Ness on September 28, about to embark on a 26-mile underwater marathon wearing a 1940s diving suit that weighs well over 100 pounds. The trek took 12 days to complete and was "far more difficult" for the Englishman than the aboveground marathons he had already run in the suit. Scott is a leukemia survivor and does these things to raise money for kids with the disease. As for Nessie, the oft-sighted but never authenticated denizen of the lake, Scott said that one day "I felt like something had grabbed my foot." Turned out it was an oil drum.

**Photograph by Christopher Furlong**
Reuters

**❝ Cold and very lonely. ❞**

— **Lloyd Scott,** describing his stint in the murky depths of Loch Ness

**Sept. 23** Scientists report that the 150-square-mile, 100-foot-thick **Ward Hunt Ice Shelf,** the Arctic's largest, has broken into two parts off the northern coast of Canada. The giant mass, which has been in place for 3,000 years, also calved massive ice blocks quite capable of damaging ships. Accelerated local warming as well as changes in the Arctic Ocean are blamed for the breakdown.

**Sept. 23** President Bush addresses world leaders at the 58th annual plenary session of the United Nations General Assembly and receives a chilly response. He seeks **aid for Iraq** by asking other nations for assistance in rebuilding the war-torn country. Other speakers rebuke the U.S. for going into Iraq without the U.N.

# FOCUS ON The Blackout

On the afternoon of August 14, the largest blackout in North American history left 50 million in the U.S. and Canada without power. And then, dusk began to fall.

**The Long Walk Home**
In a scene eerily reminiscent of September 11, New Yorkers straggle across the Brooklyn Bridge. In fact, anxiety in the city is so acute after the juice goes off, authorities rush to assure that this isn't another terrorist attack. (Later, blame will be placed on outdated transmission systems.) Fears assuaged, New Yorkers pitch in by hosting out-of-towners or serving as volunteer traffic cops. Some view the calm and kindness as the real September 11 legacy.

Chad Rachman

Steve Liss

**Snow Day in Summer**
Gotham, with its elevators,
subways and skyline, gets the
press, but from Detroit and
Toronto east to Massachusetts,
people suffer without lights,
air conditioning or even water
for days. Above, a doctor in
Cleveland uses a flashlight to
treat a patient with a collapsed
lung. Toronto residents beat
the heat with ice cream.
Barbers in Bridgeport, Conn.,
use natural light, and will rely
on the sun's warmth as a dryer.

Ron Antonelli/ReflexNews

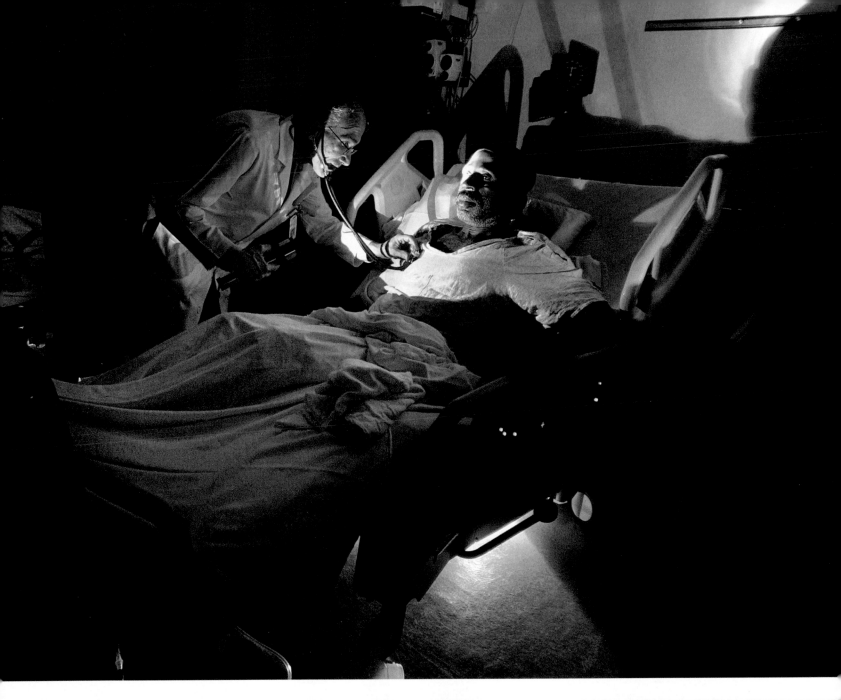

David Lucas/Reuters

Dan Herrick/Zuma

### Gloom Goes Global

North America was not alone in the dark. Subsequent to the stateside blackout, England, Italy, Denmark and Sweden all experienced their own power failures, with causes ranging from faulty transmission lines to a felled tree. On August 28, in London (above), when electricity is lost for 40 minutes during the evening rush hour, a quarter million commuters get stuck in the tube. On September 28, in Rome (left), the shutdown hit at 3:30 a.m. The timing might be considered convenient, were this not Notte Bianca—the white, or sleepless, night: The festival, intended to keep the city hopping till dawn with performances and light displays, is thoroughly undermined by steady rains and the knockout blow of the blackout. One dejected reveler, Massimiliano Bellocchi, speaks for many: "The white night? It's more like the dark night."

Alessia Pierdomenico/Reuters; inset: Kpix

# PORTRAIT | **Tony Blair**

Defying many of his countrymen, he allied Great Britain firmly with the U.S. and led the charge into Iraq. All year long, he paid for his decision. Photographs by Nick Danziger

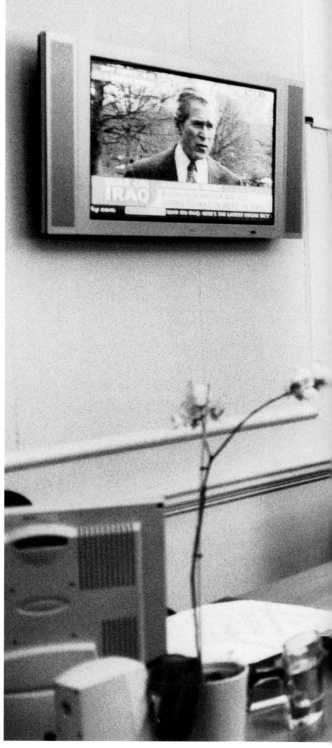

**On a flight from England to the U.S., Blair is grilled about what role the U.N. should play in postwar Iraq. Below, after a telephone negotiation with Yasir Arafat, Blair confers with his staff. Alastair Campbell is standing.**

On the last day of 2002, the BBC predicted for Tony Blair that 2003 was "likely to be his most difficult year yet as prime minister." The British economy was sputtering; Blair's Labor Party was being roundly criticized for failing to improve public services; firefighters were threatening strikes nationwide; efforts toward peace in Northern Ireland were going poorly; higher taxes were imminent. And: "The spectre of war in Iraq

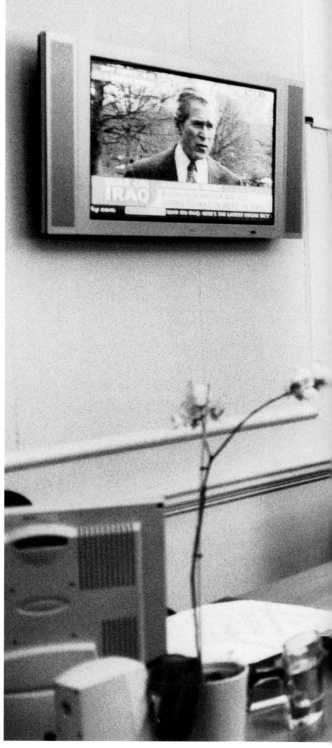

Contact Press (5)

casts the greatest shadow." Mobilization of the British military was under way, and there was every indication that Blair would throw in with whatever action the United States took against Iraq, despite the fact that many—even most—Britons vehemently opposed any war.

Everything the BBC foresaw came to pass, particularly the assertion that 2003 would be a year of severe trial for Blair. Before the U.S. attacked Baghdad in March, Blair made it clear that Great Britain, in stark contrast to fellow European powers France and Germany, would be part of the campaign. There were massive prewar protests in London, and lesser demonstrations once the conflict began. While the war itself served to bolster President Bush's standing in the States, and while its messy, drawn-out aftermath did not immediately erode his support, the opposite was true in England. The BBC and others started questioning whether, in fact, the Blair administration had exaggerated the dangers

**Bush's fate and his own were inextricably linked every moment, all year long. In the outer office of Number 10 Downing Street, Blair grimaces as Bush announces that several U.S. soldiers have been captured.**

**At Camp David, the President and the PM are in step; where each man is headed is yet unknown. In London, the father of four relaxes outside his children's bedroom. Such quiet moments, which were rare in 2003, will be equally elusive in '04.**

of Iraq's weapons program in order to justify its role in the war. Blair, his high-profile press secretary Alastair Campbell and others were called to answer by press and parliament. Dr. David Kelly, Britain's top expert on biological weapons, committed suicide after giving testimony. Blair hung on, but Campbell resigned in late August, all the while insisting his action had nothing to do with any investigations, whether into government misrepresentations or, now, Kelly's death.

Going forward, Tony Blair is lucky; his opposition is largely in disarray. Still, his own government is now seen as suspect and vulnerable. The drumbeat for new elections will surely intensify in 2004. As two who rode together into Iraq, Bush and Blair, ramp up their campaigns in the next several months, the BBC predicts another tough year for Tony Blair.

# Fall

# Moondance

As we all know, our moon produces no light of its own and must instead rely on the sun for illumination. When the earth passes precisely between a full moon and the sun, the earth's umbral shadow cloaks the moon, and creates a total lunar eclipse. It is the sort of all-too-rare timeless event that imbues us with the same awe once felt by the ancients. Here, a photographic treatment that was taken on November 9 in Connecticut.

**Photograph by Michael Melford**

## Old-timer's Game

Baseball's postseason playoffs proved to be rollicking and riveting. The long-accursed Boston Red Sox and Chicago Cubs were in the tournament, so sentimentalists everywhere tuned in. When a fan reached for a foul ball in Chitown's Wrigley Field, the Florida Marlins suddenly had new life—and took advantage of it, winning the National League pennant. Meantime, the series between Boston and the archrival New York Yankees was rock 'em, sock 'em, never more so than when 72-year-old Yankees coach Don Zimmer, furious at 31-year-old Red Sox ace Pedro Martinez for throwing at a Yankee batter, took on Martinez during a bench-clearing brawl. Pedro deflected Zim's charge, and the old guy went down. So, eventually, did the Red Sox—painfully, in seven games. Then the *who-are-they?* Marlins beat the Yanks in the World Series.

**Photograph by CJ Gunther** EPA

" I'm embarrassed. "

— **Don Zimmer**

**Oct. 3** On his 59th birthday, Roy Horn, half of the illusionist team of Siegfried & Roy, is **mauled and dragged off the stage** by a 600-pound white tiger at the Mirage casino in Las Vegas. Horn survives several operations and slowly recovers.

**Oct. 6** The Nobel Prize for Physiology or Medicine is awarded to American Paul C. Lauterbur, 74, and Briton Sir Peter Mansfield, 69, for their work on magnetic resonance imaging, or **MRI.** More than 60 million MRIs are performed every year.

Filippo Monteforte/EPA

## Giants of the Church

On October 19, some 250,000 faithful jam into and around St. Peter's Square at the Vatican for the beatification ceremony of the late Mother Teresa, the nun whose work among Calcutta's poor earned her the Nobel Peace Prize. Pope John Paul II presided at the service only three days after another Mass commemorating his 25th anniversary as leader of the Roman Catholic Church. Both affairs were joyous but poignant, as the 83-year-old pontiff, who suffers from Parkinson's disease, was clearly frail, at times barely able to speak.

**Photograph by Alberto Pizzoli** Polaris

**Oct. 10** Admitting that he is **addicted to painkillers,** Rush Limbaugh, 52, takes a leave of absence and checks into rehab. Five weeks later, the radio host tells his listeners that prosecutors obtained his medical records in "a fishing expedition."

**Oct. 10** Christopher Paolini, 19, of Paradise Valley, Mont., is giving J.K. Rowling a run for her money. His novel, *Eragon,* the first of a trilogy, is a fantasy tale that has been on *The New York Times* list of **best-selling kids' books** for a month. Late in the year, *Eragon* was still a hot item.

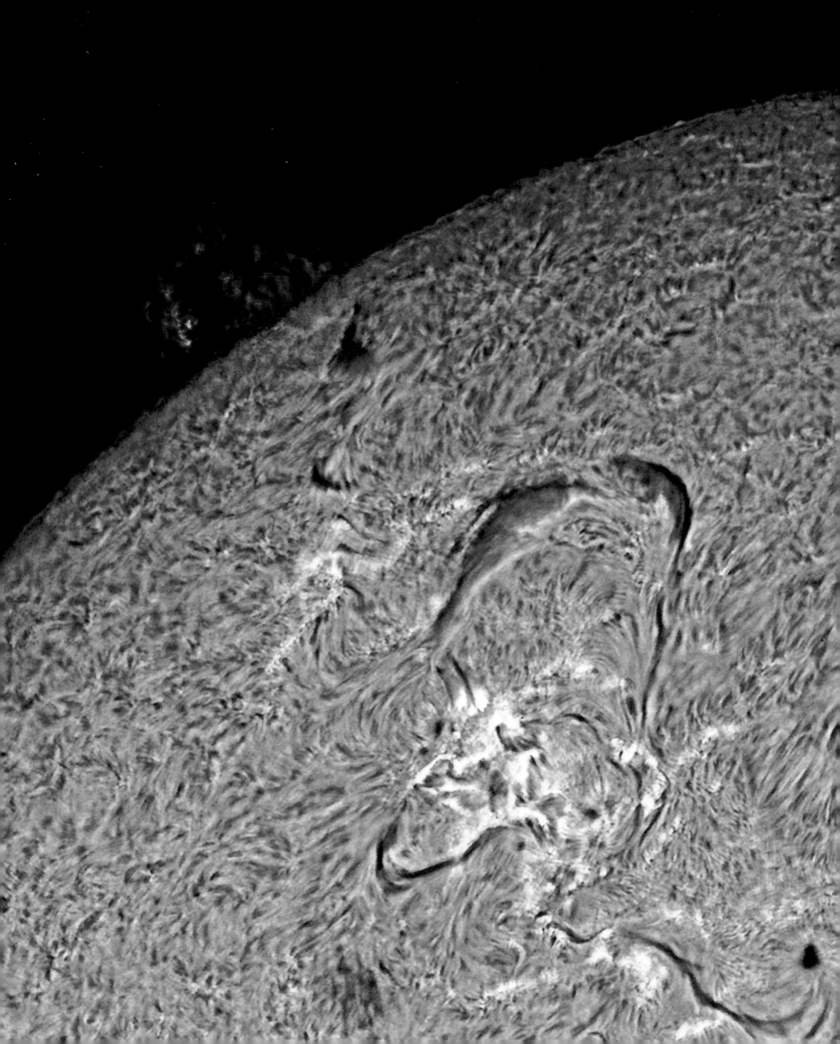

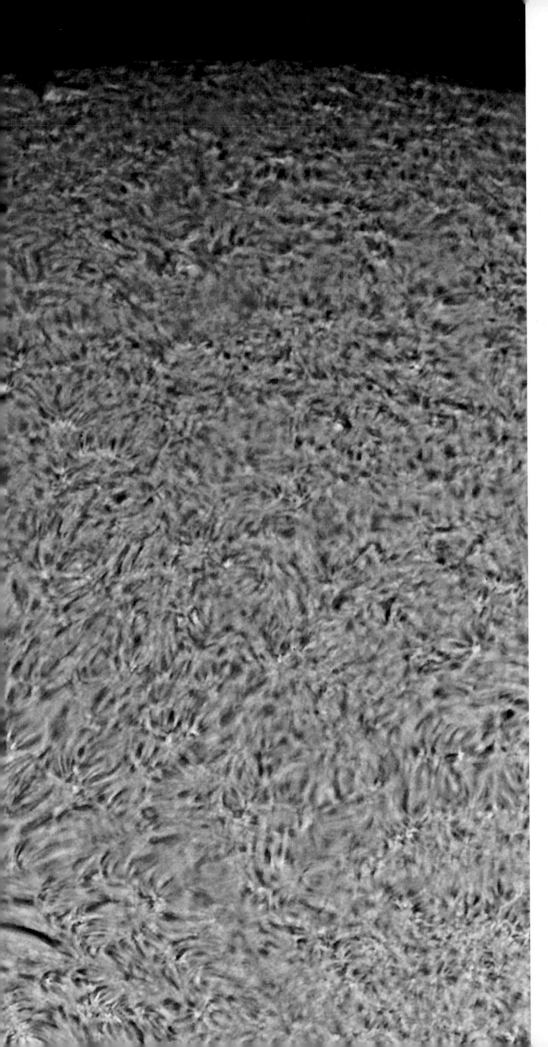

## The Sun God Is Angry

This season witnessed some of the most violent solar explosions in the recorded history of our star. The torrents of burning plasma, caused by unusual sunspot activity, began in earnest in October and continued through early November. Scientists have their own vocabulary for solar phenomena, thus on November 4 they noted that sunspot 486 had unleashed an X28 flare, the most powerful ever known. There had been fears these solar storms might affect airplanes, computers, cell phones, even the firefighting activities in California, but in the end, they remained a matter of importance only to scientists and sun worshipers.

**Photograph by Jack Newton**

**Oct. 15** Eleven people are killed and dozens injured when **a Staten Island ferry crashes** into a pier. The well-known transport system, which carries 18 million people a year, has long been considered very safe. Questions arise as to the whereabouts of the captain at the time of the accident.

**Oct. 15** Yang Liwei, 38, aboard **Chinese spacecraft** *Shenzhou 5,* blasts off alone from the Gobi Desert. After completing 14 orbits, he touches down in Inner Mongolia with one regret: "The scenery was very beautiful. But I did not see the Great Wall."

**Oct. 20** The D.C.-area sniper trials open in Virginia Beach. John A. Muhammad fires his lawyers and tells the jury: "I had nothing to do with the crime." Two days later, he rehires his lawyers. He is found **guilty** of murder on November 17 and is sentenced to death a week later.

# The Lady Is a Champ

When Julie Krone retired in 1999, winning three races at a meet in Grand Prairie, Tex., she felt she had nothing left to achieve. She was already the first woman to win a race at a major U.S. track, and the first to win a Triple Crown event (the Belmont Stakes in 1993). She had 3,545 wins in an 18-year career, ranking 16th all-time in earnings with more than $81 million. She had indeed done it all. But the lure of racing was too great for the Hall of Fame jockey, and she returned in 2002, then again in '03 after breaking bones in her lower back. Here on October 25, Krone, on Halfbridled (far right), is soon to be the first woman to win a Breeders' Cup race.

**Photograph by Bill Frakes**
Sports Illustrated

**❝ As an athlete, I have an insurmountable amount of desire. I'm ruthless, cocky, self-assured and almost always unbeatable. ❞**

—**Julie Krone**

**Oct. 20**  With only the clothes on his back, Kirk Jones, 40, of Canton, Mich., cascades 173 feet down the Canadian Horseshoe Falls at Niagara. He is the first adult known to have **survived the plunge** unaided. It is not a stunt; Jones was feeling suicidal.

**Oct. 21**  Producer David Gest, 50, the estranged husband of 57-year-old Liza Minnelli, files a civil suit against her, citing spousal abuse. He sues for $10 million, accusing her of drinking and violence: **"The alcohol gave her remarkable force and strength."** Minnelli denies the charges and is seeking a divorce.

Bob Strong/Reuters

## To Be As Two

"At one point, when someone came up and said you have two boys, the father jumped to my neck and he hugged me, and he fainted and I cared for him," recounts an Egyptian physician who had treated two-year-old conjoined twins Mohamed (left) and Ahmed Ibrahim. The joy felt by their father after the October surgery at Children's Medical Center in Dallas resonated throughout the world. Things did not go as well in July when 29-year-old Iranian twins died on the operating table in Singapore. Ladan (above, left) and Laleh Bijani knew the odds of success were only 50-50, but felt it was worth the risk to have a chance to lead their own lives.

**Photograph by Mei-Chun Jau**
Dallas Morning News/Corbis

**Oct. 24** The Concorde embarks on its **final flight.** The needle-nosed plane carries 100 guests who sip champagne, munch on lobster fishcakes and talk of Michelangelo as they cross the Atlantic in a few hours.

## Look, Ma—No Hands!

Jazi, an East African river hippopotamus, may be only three months old, but that doesn't mean she can't get around. These tubby little kids are happy underwater from the get-go. Here, in a pool at the San Diego Zoo in October, mama Funani nudges along her 260-pound daughter. A young hippo will often climb onto its mother's back and sun while she floats along. In the wild, hippos live for about 40 years, while in a zoo they can reach age 50—that is, with the right mothering.

**Photograph by Ken Bohn** San Diego Zoo

**Oct. 31** A TV crew covering the Robert Blake murder trial suddenly turns its cameras on William Strier, 64, as he opens fire on 53-year-old attorney Gerald Curry outside a courthouse in Van Nuys, Calif. Although **the lawyer is shot** several times as he hides behind a tree and tries to dodge the bullets, it is remarkable that he survives a prolonged gun attack at point-blank range with no serious damage.

**Nov. 2** After much discord, Gene Robinson, 56, is consecrated as the first **openly gay** Episcopal bishop, in Durham, N.H.

**Nov. 5** "I killed so many women I have a hard time keeping them straight," says Gary Ridgway, 54, as he pleads guilty to murdering 48 women beginning in the 1980s. Called the **Green River Killer** for the area in Washington where he committed the murders, Ridgway, a truck driver in Seattle, is the deadliest serial killer ever to be convicted in the U.S.

**Nov. 11** Multimillionaire Robert Durst, 60, is **acquitted of murder** despite admitting to dismembering a neighbor and depositing the pieces in Galveston Bay. Durst remains in jail for jumping bail.

## Terror

Less than one week after blasts at two synagogues in Istanbul killed 25 people, the city was shocked by two bombs that went off nearly simultaneously at the British consulate and a British bank. These explosions claimed at least 32 lives, including that of the consul general, and wounded more than 450. And while all four bombings were linked to al-Qaeda—they came on the eve of President Bush's visit to Great Britain—most of the victims were Turkish Muslims. Their country was likely chosen because it is a secular (if mostly Muslim) democracy, with ties to America, Israel and the U.K. Said one veteran Turkish journalist: "It's our 9/11."

**Photograph by Kudret Topcu** AP

**❝ Let us not be lily-livered about what is going on. Not enough people in Islam are prepared to stand up and say 'enough is enough.' ❞**

—**The Reverend Ian Sherwood,**
British consulate chaplain

**Nov. 15** A gangplank leading to the *Queen Mary 2,* the **world's largest passenger ship,** collapses, killing 15 at a shipyard in St. Nazaire, France. Visitors, ready to tour the ship, fall from a height of 50 feet.

**Nov. 27** "I was just looking for a warm meal somewhere," President Bush tells stunned soldiers awaiting **Thanksgiving** dinner in the Bob Hope Dining Facility at Baghdad International Airport.

**Dec. 2** For 40 years, Lynn Wagner, 53, of Mifflin County, Pa., has been **pinching pennies**—a million of them. Thirty-seven bucketfuls of the coins nets him $10,060.

## Once Bitten, Twice Brave

On Halloween morning, surfing prodigy Bethany Hamilton, 13, lost an arm to a shark while surfing off Kauai, Hawaii. The 16-inch bite mark in her board, held above by firefighter Tim Terrazas, prompts experts to believe it was a tiger shark that was up to 15 feet long and weighed one ton. At right, just weeks later, she is back with her inseparable friend and surfing buddy Alana Blanchard, this time on a skateboard. By Thanksgiving, Bethany, who lives with her surfer parents in a community of like-minded folks, was back in the water pursuing her dream of being the best in the world. One neighbor marveled most accurately: "That girl has saltwater in her veins."

**Photograph by Chris Usher** Apix

**Dec. 12  Keiko,** the killer whale who starred in the *Free Willy* films, dies of pneumonia in the Norwegian fjord where he lived after efforts to return him to the wild failed.

**Dec. 12**  It's **knight-dubbing time** in Merrie Olde England, and today the Rolling Stones lead singer, a 60-year-old bloke named Jagger, becomes Sir Mick. Asked if he deserves the honor, he answers, "Yeah."

**Dec. 13**  Saddam Hussein is **captured.**

# FOCUS ON | California

The Golden State was sizzling all fall, with recall elections, sensational court trials, even more sensational arrests and, soberingly, real flames. The tabloid news was so outré, it nearly diverted attention from the real, human drama.

### In the Inferno

The rash of blazes in October and early November was ferocious in tenacity and destruction. Fires broke out in several places—it wasn't one east-to-west or north-to-south sweep—and finally scorched nearly three quarters of a million acres, consuming 3,650 homes. Twenty-two people were killed. Blame was cast on drought, a beetle infestation that had killed trees and made detritus susceptible to fire, and homeowners disobeying a state law requiring the removal of brush and tinder. Left: Smoke rises over Simi Valley. Above: volunteer Lee Bennette in San Diego County.

David Hume Kennerly

**The Circus Encamps**

There are plenty of fires on the Great Plains, and any place can land a spicy trial, but this was the one that had the rest of America saying, "Only in California." There, a campaign was mounted to have the electorate admit it had made a mistake by choosing Gray Davis to govern, and to apply a bizarre law to admit this mistake and force a recall referendum. This the voters

did, at which point all comers—from former child star Gary Coleman (far left) to porn king Larry Flynt (center) to porn queen Mary Carey (above) to *Doonesbury*'s Zonker—135 in all, threw their hats into the ring. Film god Arnold Schwarzenegger announced his candidacy on *The Tonight Show,* then bunkered with aides to plot a campaign (which spent much energy answering charges of sexual harrassment and a fondness for fascism). Ahhnold won handily (left, with wife Maria Shriver).

David Hume Kennerly; insets, left to right:
Paul Chinn/San Francisco Chronicle/Corbis; Lucy Nicholson/Reuters; Carlo Allegri/Getty

David Hume Kennerly

Al Golub/The Modesto Bee/AP

## Extreme Makeover

Laci Peterson was 27 years old and eight months pregnant when she disappeared on Christmas Eve, 2002. Her remains washed ashore nearly four months later. Above: When Laci's husband, Scott, a fertilizer salesman, is arrested by Modesto police on April 18 on suspicion of murder, he wears a forlorn aspect. By the time he appears in court in the autumn, he is a changed man (right, with lawyer Mark Geragos, during arraignment proceedings on December 3). Late in the year, filming began on a TV movie, *The Perfect Husband,* about the case. Dean Cain, ex of the series *Lois & Clark: The New Adventures of Superman,* will play Scott Peterson.

Pool/Reuters

## Glove's Off

Whether the case against Michael Jackson on charges of molesting a 12-year-old boy proves to be a climactic chapter in a strange, often troubled life, or the product of a vendetta by a district attorney who could not nail Jackson on similar allegations 10 years ago, will be determined by events that will unfold after Jackson's arraignment. All that is now known is that, on November 19, Santa Barbara County D.A. Thomas Sneddon Jr. issued a warrant for Jackson's arrest and barked into the cameras, "Get over here and get checked in." This Jackson does (right), setting off a media feeding frenzy unseen since O.J. Simpson. Above: Earlier in the year, in a controversial television special, Jackson admits that he has sometimes had sleepovers with children.

Jeff Chiu/AP; inset: Granada/ABC

# Mickey Mouse

There have been many stars through the years, even some deserving of the title "superstar." But no other luminary has ever been able to generate the kind of adoration—and serious lucre—that has accrued to this grand old friend.

With his first flick, *Steamboat Willie,* he hit the big time. When you compare this with the studio still from 1935 at right, it's clear they wanted him to develop a button nose and softer, rounder features, as these were considered cuddlier and, thereby, easier to love.

On November 18, one of the world's most beloved entertainers turned 75, but that did not mean he was ready to pick up his watch and crawl off into retirement. (Of course if he had, he would have been the first employee ever to receive a watch with an image of himself emblazoned on it.)

Mickey Mouse could do it all: sing, dance, act funny, act sad. He broke into show business in 1928 when he electrified the world as the lead in *Steamboat Willie,* the first successful animated film with dialogue and sound effects. At the time, he was much thinner, and his face even had, in the words of some of his critics, a rather ratlike aspect. Over the years, though, plenty of moolah under his belt led to the improved appearance that proper nutrition can give you. There were, as well, the usual

nips and tucks one expects with an elite celebrity. And when you throw in the gifted makeup crew at his studio, Disney, you end up with a dapper little bon vivant.

Mr. Mouse's agent—some say his Svengali—was Walt Disney, who with a collaborator, Ub Iwerks, helped shape him into the character beloved by all. Disney grew up in the Midwest, and the values inculcated there always informed Mr. Mouse's scripts, and his persona from one film to the next rarely varied. Mickey certainly had range, but as with, say, Gary Cooper, you always knew what you were getting.

There are those who contend that the younger Mickey—and he insists that even strangers call him that—the brasher Mickey, brought more to the screen than the affable, uncomplicated fellow he became. But as Mr. Mouse pointed out in his 1967

autobiography, *The Big Cheese?,* he shouldered a lot of responsibility. After all, the entire company was built around him. It would have been the easiest thing, he noted, to demand the meaty roles given to villains (he is known to have craved Jack Palance's role in *Shane*), but thousands of families depended on him for their weekly paycheck. It is

**When Disney saw the impact Mickey had on folks, he left no stone unturned in his quest to wring every penny out of the little guy.**

also known that now, even as his position in the company increasingly turns toward that of figure-head—despite denials from Disney—Mickey is, as always, taking it like a mouse.

No one ever doubted that Mr. Mouse was a team player. Yet he never sought publicity, even as he bailed out one colleague after another. It is a well-

**The Mickey Mouse Club** was big with baby boomers. Here, in 1955, host Jimmie and three Mouseketeers. Annette Funicello was a major attraction. At left, Mr. Mouse in *Fantasia*.

known secret in Tinseltown that, without the help of Mr. Mouse, Donald Duck would never have reemerged from the crackup that ensued when his fabulously wealthy Uncle Scrooge stiffed the aquatic one in his will.

So, this great star soldiers on at 75. And with Mr. Mouse, stride for stride as always through the years, is his beloved partner Minnie. She makes only the occasional film appearance these days, as is also the case with her Mickey. No matter—he has already given the world more than a hundred shorts, and, of course, his full-length masterwork, *Fantasia*. In 2004, Disney will release *Three Musketeers*. Kids everywhere, of every age, are hoping it will be a huge, furry hit.

Hepburn. Cash. Peck. Hope. Rogers . . . Mister Rogers. It was a year of losing giants. As we bid them farewell, we celebrate their specialness.

## Bob Hope

This quintessential American entertainer was born Leslie Townes Hope in England, and over the decades his celebrity extended to a dizzying number of spheres. He came to the U.S. as a child and soon changed his name to Bob because it sounded more "Hiya, fellas." That alteration starts to tell the story of the man who, regardless of the medium, was always Bob Hope: a self-deprecating, brash launcher of one-liners, Ol' Ski Nose, with a well-crafted sneer that lasted as long as the laugh, then, "But I wanna tell ya," the next joke, the eyebrows up, the golf club twirling . . . this was a timeless master of comedy. He had big hits on Broadway, and began a long radio career in the '30s. He made over 50 movies— highlighted by the seven *Road* movies with his pal Bing Crosby—and was a box office smash for years. He also hosted the Oscars broadcast 18 times. He did 284 TV specials for NBC and put up some serious Nielsen numbers (in 1969 he had six of the 11 top-rated shows). His annual golf tournament is one of the premier PGA Tour events. In 1941 he began to entertain American troops and he never stopped, despite some dangerous moments. His detractors said he lacked depth, but that was the beauty of Bob Hope. Nothing complex, he just wanted to make people laugh. He was survived by Dolores, his wife of 69 years, when he died at 100.

Francis Miller

Ernest Bachrach/MPTV

## Katharine Hepburn

She was a completely one-of-a-kind actor, whose every performance was infused with her particular grace, her intelligence, her dignity and her airs. She could float through a scene like a fairy princess pirouetting through chiffon. She could command a moment with an intensity that was as no-nonsense as a laser. Or she could be as down-to-earth as a tweed jacket on a drizzly spring day. And for these special gifts, she received a dozen Oscar nominations (a record equaled only this year by Meryl Streep) and brought home four statuettes. The love of her life was, famously, Spencer Tracy, but he could never divorce his wife. Still, their romance inspirited nine movies, sparkling concoctions in which their affection was entirely tangible. Of course, there were other films for this Bryn Mawr alumna. In the screwball farce *Bringing Up Baby,* she drove Cary Grant nuts. The two met again in *The Philadelphia Story.* She was a prim spinster opposite Humphrey Bogart in *The African Queen,* and in 1981's *On Golden Pond* she doted on her aging husband, played by Henry Fonda. Broadway, too, was a site for many successes. There was no one else at all like Kate, who finally yielded, for the first and last time, at 96.

Ken Regan/Camera5

## June Carter Cash and Johnny Cash

As one of Mother Maybelle Carter's three singing daughters, the little girl from Maces Spring, Va., was country music royalty—and knew it. "When I grow up," she said when she was 12, "I'm going to dine with queens." From the 1930s through the '50s, her strong, clear voice became familiar coast to coast through her many appearances on radio shows including the Grand Ole Opry's. In 1961 she hit the road for $500 a week, touring with a sharecropper's son from Kingsland, Ark., the rockabilly star Johnny Cash. In 1963 she co-wrote a hit for him, "Ring of Fire," an autobiographical song about the tempestuousness of their love affair. The Man in Black proposed onstage in 1968, and the long marriage of June and John, during which she saw him through periods of harrowing drug addiction and out of which came hit songs ("Jackson") and Grammy Awards, was a Nashville ballad truer than anything played on the radio. As a solo act, Johnny Cash was a country and TV superstar whose late-in-life renaissance produced some of his finest music and solidified his position as an American icon. June died in May at 73, and there was speculation John might follow her quickly. He did, in September, at 71.

## Hume Cronyn

He was born in Ontario in 1911 and nearly made Canada's Olympic boxing team in 1932. The ring, however, couldn't contain this intense, devilishly bright chap who was a talented writer and theatrical performer but who also made his mark in movies. A scene-stealer of exquisite precision, he was timid in *The Seventh Cross*, relentless in *Shadow of a Doubt*, wicked in *Brute Force* and endearing in *Cocoon*. In 1994 he lost his frequent acting partner and beloved wife of five decades, Jessica Tandy.

## Gregory Peck

No other leading man could convey the ironclad dignity that defined Peck, even as an outlaw (*Yellow Sky*) or a Nazi (*The Boys from Brazil*). Decency, vulnerability and inner resolve flowed from this tall man with the soft baritone and the matinee-idol looks. He starred in dozens of top-flight films, from *Twelve O'Clock High* and *The Gunfighter* through *Roman Holiday* and *Gentleman's Agreement*. For many, he is best remembered for 1962's *To Kill a Mockingbird*, in which his small-town Southern lawyer personified courage. "I put everything I had into it," he said, "everything I'd learned in 46 years of living." Peck died at 87.

## Robert Stack

As actors go, he was a bit stingy with the emotions, but there was a solidity to him that paved the way to a 60-year career. Born to ease in L.A. in 1919, he was a national skeet-shooting champion in the '30s. At Clark Gable's suggestion he tried Tinseltown, and showed well early in 1940's *The Mortal Storm*, then consented when a makeup man wanted to blacken his curly blond locks. He went on to make a lot of flicks, and sometimes shone, notably as a dissolute playboy in *Written on the Wind* (1956). His legacy, though, began to be forged in 1959 when he became Eliot Ness in the pounding TV crime classic *The Untouchables*. That unyielding persona provided a late plum: a 14-year run as host of *Unsolved Mysteries*.

## Charles Bronson

In a trade dominated by people with dreamy-pretty faces, he himself said, "I guess I look like a rock quarry that someone has dynamited." But he was also aware of his soulfulness: "I supply a presence." That intense presence was there from the start; for years he was stalwart (*The Magnificent Seven*) and even capable of depth (*Rider on the Rain*). After his turn as a vigilante widower in 1974's *Death Wish*, he megastarred in one international hit after another, some of them quite good, like *Telefon* and *Hard Times*, the latter also featuring his longtime wife, Jill Ireland. Perhaps he was best summed up by John Huston, who called Bronson "a grenade with the pin pulled." He was 81.

John Bryson

## Gregory Hines

"I don't remember not dancing," he once said, which was understandable since he learned as a toddler from his older brother, Maurice Jr. They began performing together when Gregory was five, and the following year did two weeks at the Apollo. Down the line there would be many more shows, often with his brother (sometimes with Dad on drums), including some devastating star turns on Broadway in the likes of *Eubie* and *Jelly's Last Jam,* for which he copped a Tony. The premier tapper of his time, he also appeared in movies and had a recurring role on *Will & Grace.* A beloved man, he died of liver cancer at 57.

## Donald O'Connor

He was born to vaudevillians in 1925. "I was about 13 months old, they tell me, when I first started dancing. And they'd hold me up by the back of my neck and they'd start the music and I would dance . . . You could do that with any kid, only I got paid for it." And he stayed a pro through a lifetime of dancing, acting and singing, ever easy with a smile—even in six films opposite a talking mule. His time-capsule moment came with his brilliant "Make 'Em Laugh" performance in *Singin' in the Rain.*

Hulton Archive/Getty

Black Star

## Elia Kazan

One of the greatest theatrical directors of modern times as well as a master of cinema, this Greek immigrant used intelligence and passion to secure blistering performances in such classics as, onstage, *Death of a Salesman* and *Streetcar,* and onscreen, *A Face in the Crowd* and *On the Waterfront*. But while his artistry was memorable, also unforgettable for many was that in 1952 he named names at a government hearing on communism. Orson Welles said that he "traded his soul for a swimming pool." Said Kazan: "There's a normal sadness about hurting people, but I'd rather hurt them a little than hurt myself a lot." He was 94.

## Leni Riefenstahl

"It seemed as if the earth's surface were spreading out before me, like a hemisphere that suddenly splits apart in the middle . . . I felt paralyzed." That is how Riefenstahl described the first time she heard Adolf Hitler speak. Her reputation as a peerless documentary filmmaker is based on two efforts, *Olympia* in 1938 and, more to the point, *Triumph of the Will,* for which her artistic breakthroughs were lauded, while she herself was castigated for mythologizing the 1934 Nazi rally in Nuremberg. She claimed, right up to her death at age 101, to have been guilty only of depicting Germany as it was at the time.

WRC·TV·CHANNEL 4

NBC

NBC/Globe Photos

Jim Judkis

## David Brinkley

Born in Wilmington, N.C., in 1920, he began his journalistic career as a teen at a local paper. After serving in the war, he went to Washington, D.C., and became NBC's first White House correspondent. Along the way, he began appearing on a new medium that was taking hold: television. In the mid-'50s he was paired with Chet Huntley, and the latter's straightforward delivery blended seamlessly with Brinkley's offhand, droll manner. The duo's nightly news broadcast topped the ratings till the late '60s. Brinkley's Sunday-morning show was a fixture on ABC from 1981 to 1997. Throughout, his unassailable integrity suffused his wry yet endearing manner to provide, in essence, a national conscience.

Neal Peters Collection

## Art Carney

"The first time I saw the guy act, I knew I would have to work twice as hard for my laughs. He was funny as hell." So said Jackie Gleason, Carney's partner on *The Honeymooners,* the '50s TV classic in which his laid-back, seemingly dim-witted Ed Norton was a foil to Gleason's volcanic Ralph Kramden. Carney's long, fidgeting takes that would render Gleason ballistic are among comedy's priceless moments. His classic timing earned Carney, who suffered from a limp as a result of D-Day shrapnel, an Oscar for 1974's *Harry and Tonto.* He was 85.

## Fred Rogers

Mister Rogers was a persona, but he was also a very real person—as real as they come.
Fred Rogers, the gentle puppeteer and Presbyterian minister from Pennsylvania, could
visit the country's children in character, wearing that sweater and bearing that dead-ahead
gaze, but if he didn't tell them the truth on a daily basis, they would have had little use for
him. As it was, generations of Americans learned about values and hope and travail—how
to deal with divorcing parents, how to deal with September 11—from their special mentor-
friend. It was a sad day in the neighborhood when Mister Rogers died at 74.

## John Ritter

His frenetic but ingratiating manner suited him perfectly for the role of Jack Tripper in *Three's Company*, a silly sitcom that ran from 1977 to 1984 and was one of television's highest-rated shows of all time. He parlayed that character into a slew of TV appearances that cemented his reputation as one of the most likable guys to appear on the little screen. A Hollywood High grad, and the son of legendary country-and-western singer-actor Tex Ritter, John died suddenly at age 54 of a coronary-artery tear. It was his daughter Stella's fifth birthday.

## Buddy Ebsen

He was adept at many phases of show biz, and might have found even greater fame: His gangly, cartoonish dancing made him ideal for the Tin Man role in *The Wizard of Oz*, but as it happened he was allergic to the metallic makeup (Jack Haley got the part). A veteran of vaudeville, movies and theater, Ebsen became a fixture on TV. First he was Davy Crockett's sidekick, Georgie, then he struck pay dirt as Jed Clampett, the benign patriarch on *The Beverly Hillbillies;* for most of the '70s he starred in the hit *Barnaby Jones*. His folksy manner may not have wowed the critics, but everyone else thought he was aces. Ebsen was 95.

## Buddy Hackett

Brash, bright, boyish Buddy was born in Brooklyn and emerged from New York's Borscht Belt to appear in every major nightclub in America and on countless TV shows. He also garnered solid notices for his efforts onstage and in movies. In his stand-up work, he would go off on a topic, invariably ribald, in that odd delivery he had mastered, and take flight like a gooney bird. And if he got into a groove, which he often did, he was the kind of comic who could make an audience laugh convulsively. He died in Malibu at age 78.

## Barry White

Known alternately as the Buddha of the Bedroom and the Black Walrus of Love, this maestro of the deep, coaxing voice that was immersed in opulent, libidinous arrangements sold more than 100 million records, mostly in his '70s disco heyday and during a recent comeback. He didn't so much sing as plead and promise, while attesting to his considerable romantic powers in songs like "Can't Get Enough of Your Love, Babe." Kidney failure finally felled him at 58. "He had his family around him," said an associate. "They knew he was going. He died peacefully."

Everett Collection

## Hank Ballard

He was discovered singing on the assembly line at a Ford plant, and in 1954 he and his group, soon to be known as the Midnighters, had a million-seller called "Work with Me Annie." That a follow-up was "Annie Had a Baby" gives some idea of the content of their tunes: raw, and with an insistent beat. The Midnighters' tough instrumentation combined with Ballard's fabulous vocals for some hypnotic rock 'n' roll. In 1958, Ballard penned and recorded a song that was lost as a B side. Two years later, Chubby Checker covered it, and "The Twist" set off a national dance craze. Ballard's birth year is listed as either 1927 or 1936.

Paul Rider / Retna

such as Carl Perkins, Jerry Lee Lewis, Roy Orbison and Johnny Cash. And despite the dubious Presley deal, he ended up a rich man because he got in on the ground floor of another Memphis hit: Holiday Inn. Phillips was 80.

"You've Lost That Lovin' Feelin'," which is the most played record in radio history. Medley's raspy bass was matched by Hatfield's tenor, by turns edgy and soaring ("Ebb Tide"). He died of a heart attack at age 63, a half hour before a Righteous Brothers show.

# Nina Simone

She was born Eunice Waymon in 1933 in Tryon, N.C., and received classical training at Juilliard, but no one discipline could hold her emotional singing and piano-playing. Her smoky, intense vocals were mostly called jazz, to which she responded, "Calling me a jazz singer was a way of ignoring my musical background, because I didn't fit into white ideas of what a black performer should be." In 1973 she left the U.S. and settled in France, where she stayed for the rest of her life. A staunch civil-rights advocate, she was one of the most impassioned performers of her time.

# Benny Carter

A deeply respected jazz artist, he never caught the attention of a wider audience like other bandleaders such as Louis Armstrong or Count Basie. Born in New York City in 1907, Carter was a primary architect of swing, but was his own man: He left the U.S. for Europe in '35 and stayed for a few years—just when the music was exploding on the charts back home. His peers admired his lyrical, lilting playing and considered him, Johnny Hodges and Charlie Parker the three modern masters of alto sax. Quincy Jones summed him up perfectly: "We walked through the door on his shoulders. He was a quiet and dignified man. And one of a kind."

Alexis Rodriguez-Duarte/Corbis Outline

William Gottlieb/Retna

# Celia Cruz

"*Azúcar*!" was her trademark onstage cry, Spanish for "sugar," and this honey-throated contralto was one sweet singer and an even sweeter person. Born in Havana around 1924, the second oldest of 14 kids, she hit it big in the early '50s as a band singer, then fled Castro's regime for the U.S. in 1960. She reigned as the Queen of Salsa, working with such Latin music giants as Tito Puente and Johnny Pacheco. Since she never recorded in English, many Americans never got to see her—an awful shame because, while she was private and dignified offstage, in performance she was a whirlwind of wild wigs, flashy gowns, titanic heels, gyrating torso, and that voice . . . that voice.

Leonard McCombe

David Gahr

# Strom Thurmond

The only eight-term member in the history of the U.S. Senate, he spent a century on this earth as a vital, valorous and colorful man, a teetotaler with a fondness for pretty, young wives. The son of a lawyer, he left South Carolina in World War II and returned from D-Day as a war hero who campaigned for, and won, his state's governorship. Two years later, in 1948, his failed bid for the White House as a Dixiecrat—a group opposed to Harry Truman's civil rights platform—was a signature moment. The next five decades saw many more chapters in a career built on changing when the voters wanted change. For his own epitaph, he suggested, "He loved the people, and the people loved him."

# Daniel Patrick Moynihan

At age 10, a comfy life in New York turned to poverty when his father abandoned the family. Young Pat shined shoes after school and later worked as a stevedore and bartender (he had a lifelong yen for food and grog). This real-world tutelage informed the future social scientist who would focus on the underprivileged. He served four Presidents, including Kennedy and Nixon, and became known for his bold policy proposals. In 1976 he quit as ambassador to the U.N. and won the first of four terms in the Senate. There, once again, Moynihan was no slave to ideology, and his glib wit, prescience and scholarly passion made him, as Sen. Edward M. Kennedy noted, a paradigm "of what the Founding Fathers thought the Senate would be about." He was 76.

One of the grand, indomitable ladies of the 1900s, she was born in China in 1898, the daughter of an American-educated missionary-turned-entrepreneur. As a child she went to the U.S., where she graduated from Wellesley. Her indoctrination to the States was so thorough that she said, "The only thing Oriental about me is my face." In 1928, one year after her marriage in China, her husband became the leader of the ruling Nationalist Party. Madame Chiang was particularly conspicuous during WWII as she rallied American support for her homeland. Her husband held the reins in China till he fled to Taiwan in '49 to avoid the communists. Having lived in three centuries, she died in self-imposed exile in New York at age 105.

## Idi Amin

One of the scourges of the 20th century, this son of a farmer and a sorceress changed his country overnight from a prosperous African nation to a land of nightmares. In 1971, Amin, a general in the Ugandan army, overthrew the government of Milton Obote, triggering eight years of torture, dismemberment and murder accomplished with the likes of sledgehammers. At times the corpses so outpaced the graves that they were heaved into the Nile; by the end, perhaps half a million had been killed. Along the way, Amin also destroyed Uganda's economy. He was finally routed by Tanzanian soldiers and Ugandan exiles, and fled to Saudi Arabia with his four wives and dozens of children. He was about 80.

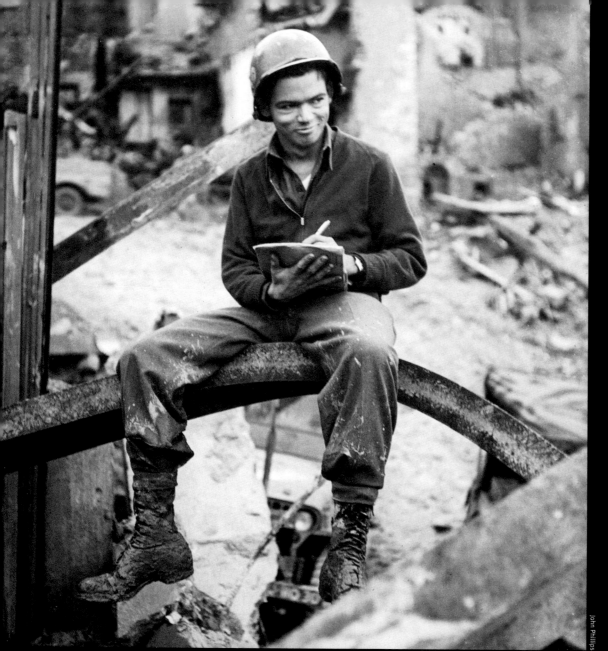

## Bill Mauldin

For American enlisted men in World War II, Betty Grable made them dream about the girls at home, but Mauldin was the one who made them laugh even as they lay in their muddy, lonely trenches. Of course, he was one of them, a rifleman in Europe, so Willie and Joe, his characters in *Stars and Stripes*, were the real thing: dog-tired dogfaces filled, in Mauldin's words, with "a deep, almost hopeless desire to go home and forget it all." Willie and Joe let GIs know that there were others who were saddled with inept officers and one lousy detail after another. Mauldin won two Pulitzers and was one of America's toughest editorial cartoonists for 50 years. He died at 81.

John Phillips

## Robert McCloskey

The native Ohioan's first book for kids, *Lentil,* was set in the Midwest, but it was his second, *Make Way for Ducklings*, a 1941 book about a family of fowl who settle in Boston's Public Garden, that secured his fame (and the first of two Caldecott Medals for the year's best picture book for children). *Ducklings* was a wild success— there are now more than two million copies in print—and has been immortalized in bronze sculptures in Boston and Moscow, Russia. Later McCloskey stories—*Blueberries for Sal, One Morning in Maine*— were autobiographical tales that took place on an island where he had settled with his family. He was 88.

## Al Hirschfeld

As a young artist, he took a trip to Bali, where the sun bleached out all color and reduced people to "walking line drawings," leading to his becoming, as he said, "enchanted with line." Thus began the career of America's legendary caricaturist, whose pen-and-ink distillations appeared on stamps and magazine covers, and graced *The New York Times* for seven decades. His daughter Nina was born in 1945, and ever after her name was tantalizingly woven into Hirschfeld's canny, breezy pictures. The Line King, who was synonymous with Broadway, was 99.

Bob Gomel

## Robert Atkins

"My English sheepdog will figure out nutrition before the dietitians do," he said in response to mainstream concerns expressed about the revolutionary diet theories espoused in his 1972 bestseller. Atkins, a cardiologist, held that if you don't eat carbs, the body will burn its own fat. And now his eat-the-bacon-cheeseburger-hold-the-bun recipe has more adherents than ever. Indeed, short-term research has suggested he may be right, though others still say there could be consequences. His fans, meanwhile, simply point to the scale and smile. In any event, death once more proved inescapable, as he died at 72 of head injuries suffered from a fall on an icy sidewalk.

Michele Asselin

## George Plimpton

The day before his death, he wrapped up the 50th-anniversary edition of *The Paris Review,* the "little magazine" he edited that became the best of the bunch. For Plimpton, this was but one hue in his kaleidoscopic life in journalism. Patrician, droll, charming and always wanting to be in the fray, he boxed with Archie Moore; played QB for the Detroit Lions; pitched to Willie Mays; served to Pancho Gonzalez; was an outlaw gunned down by John Wayne in *Rio Lobo;* played a therapist in *Good Will Hunting;* and, without any humor at all, helped subdue Sirhan Sirhan after he shot Bobby Kennedy. Plimpton was 76.

Harry Benson

Alfred Eisenstaedt

## Edward Teller

"The father of the hydrogen bomb" is a sobriquet that few would cherish. For Teller, however, the enemies were so frightening that any means justified the end. Born in Hungary, he dreaded the Nazis and the communists. When J. Robert Oppenheimer said after WWII that the atomic bomb was big enough, Teller implied that Oppenheimer was a security risk. Ironically, it was Teller who was hurt by this, and as colleague and Nobel laureate Isidor I. Rabi said: "It would have been a better world without Teller." Two decades before his death at 95, Teller reemerged to champion the Star Wars defense system for President Reagan.

## Bill Shoemaker

He weighed only two pounds when he was born, so his grandmother kept him alive by putting him in a shoebox and warming it on the kitchen stove. He finally got up to 98 pounds, small even for a jockey, but that didn't keep him from steering big, powerful horses to 8,833 wins. His fluid riding style was a thing of beauty, leading him to 11 Triple Crown victories, including the 1986 Kentucky Derby when, at age 54, he took Ferdinand to the winner's circle. "Shoe," who died of undisclosed causes at age 72, had been paralyzed from the neck down after a 1991 car crash, in which, ironically, he was driving a Bronco.

## Althea Gibson

Usually someone born to poverty in South Carolina and raised on welfare in Harlem, someone who suffered beatings at the hands of her father, would be on a dead-end track. But if someone was very special—with a character that would bend but never ever break—that someone could, without a lot of muss or fuss, become the first African American to play in a U.S. national tennis championship, and the first to win it; the first to win at Wimbledon; the first to garner five Grand Slam titles; and the first to play on the women's pro golf tour. That someone would be Althea Gibson, who died of respiratory failure at 76.

## Warren Spahn

He was born in Buffalo in 1921 to a wallpaper salesman, and, quite frankly, he looked more like a wallpaper salesman than a pitcher who would win more games than any other left-hander in history—363. He might even have won a few more had he not joined the Army in 1943 (he received a battlefield commission and was awarded a Bronze Star). Spahnnie was a guy who was liked by all. But on the mound he was deadly intent on victory. Said a former coach, "Every pitch he throws has an idea behind it." And as former pitcher Johnny Podres noted: "He was just a master of his trade. I couldn't take my eyes off him."

## Gertrude Ederle

The '20s were an era of bigger-than-life heroes. Lucky Lindy, Babe Ruth, Bill Tilden and, of course, Gertrude Ederle. In 1926, at the age of 19, she became the first woman to swim the English Channel. She did it in record time, and no woman would swim the channel faster for another 35 years. It was quite important because at the time not much thought was given to women athletes. But this "water baby," as she called herself, who grew up swimming on the New Jersey shore, helped change all that. When Ederle returned to a tremendous ticker-tape parade in New York, Mayor Jimmy Walker merely compared her feat to Moses' parting of the Red Sea.

# JUST ONE MORE

Jose Azel/Aurora

"There was the broad arch of the forehead, a hundred feet in height; the nose, with its long bridge; and the vast lips, which, if they could have spoken, would have rolled their thunder accents from one end of the valley to the other." So wrote Hawthorne in his story "The Great Stone Face," which concerned a remarkable rock outcropping in Franconia, N.H., that was better known as the Old Man of the Mountain. The very cragginess of the granite profile—its roughness, its toughness—seemed to speak of immortality, but geologists knew that the Old Man was in a precarious situation, and that even buttresses and cables installed during the 20th century didn't render him invincible. No one saw him tumble on May 3, as the canyon was filled with a thick fog. When word spread a few days later that the Old Man had succumbed to the always erosive freeze-thaw cycle, tears were general from Concord to Coos County. Though rocks may crumble, the Old Man lives on as the state emblem, on the back of a handsome quarter, on a zillion coffee mugs and souvenir pennants, in literature—and in the hearts and minds of all Granite Staters.

**Photograph by Bob LaPree**